Thank You for Drinking Beer

Essays and Stories

~*~

By Harry Schuhmacher

Copyright © 2014 by Harry Schuhmacher
All rights reserved. No part of this book may be reproduced or transmitted in any form or by any means, electronic or mechanical, including photocopying, recording, or by any information storage and retrieval system, without permission in writing from the author.

Note: This is a work of fiction, in that in many cases, the author could not remember the exact words said by certain people, and exact descriptions of certain things, so had to fill in gaps as best he could. All events described herein actually happened, though on occasion the author has taken small liberties with chronology.

SCHUHMACHER PUBLISHING, INC.
909 NE Loop 410, Suite 720
San Antonio, TX 78209
WWW.BEERNET.COM

For Wyatt, Hunt, and Harrison

"Be who you are and say what you feel, because those who mind don't matter and those who matter don't mind."

- *Dr. Seuss*

"I wish I'd had a beer."
- *Anybody who has ever had anything except beer.*

CONTENTS

~*~

Thank You for Drinking Beer	i
Hitting the Bricks	1
A Conversation with my Dog	27
The Beer-Drinking Goat	34
Beer Man in Beverly Hills	43
Getting Kicked Out of Costa Rica	64
Dolphin Rock	76

An Occupational Hazard	82
Shake n' Bake	101
Remembrance of Things Past	106
Christmas Crime	110
Farewell, O. Henry's	130
Please Come to Boston	135
I Can't See	140
Leaving Las Vegas	143

Dragons Live Forever, But Not So Little Boys	150
About the Author	153

THANK YOU FOR DRINKING BEER

NO, SERIOUSLY, THANK YOU.

For every two kegs of beer you drink, I make about half a cent. It doesn't seem like much, but when you add up all those kegs and subsequent ha' pennies, it keeps my three sons in Nikes and keeps their father as a member in good standing at the Admiral's Club, Terminal C, DFW Airport.

Those half pennies have allowed me to travel around the world visiting breweries, speak in all fifty states, send two sons through college with a third on his way, and maintain a fairly high-maintenance wife.

But it wasn't always this way. In fact, back in January of 1998, I found myself stone broke, living off what I could safely embezzle from my family, and squatting at my grandparents' ranch with two young sons and a hostile wife. If you have ever been broke with two toddlers and a hostile rib, well, then you know what kind of special hell that is.

I had married her after I graduated fresh out of the University of Texas with a promising job at a Houston beer distributorship and a nice little house (inside the Loop!).

Little did she know that seven years later, she would be living in a run-down ranch house in Leon Springs, Texas, without two nickels to rub together and two brats with snot running down their noses, and bedding an unemployed wannabe journalist with nothing but a failed attempt at Harvard and some outdated beer industry contacts. Not quite hitting bottom, but not quite the pinnacle of life when you're broaching thirty.

After taking full stock of my abilities, my professional aspirations, and my bank balance, I found inspiration in a dusty tome I thieved from my grandfather's library: *Briton Hadden: A Biography*. Hadden, along with Henry Luce, having raised a total of $86,000 from seventy-four investors, published the first issue of *TIME, The Weekly*

Newsmagazine in 1923. Luce served as business manager, and Hadden was the editor; his editorial style was eccentric and unique for that time. Above all, he strived to make all copy brief, to the point, and interesting.

Reading about Hadden gave me my ultimate "Aha!" moment: I know a lot about the beer industry, I'm a writer, and email is just starting to get widespread use. I know — I'll start a daily trade newspaper sent via email covering the U.S. beer industry, and it will be written in a simple, brief, interesting and humorous style, like Hadden had successfully tried with *TIME*.

I started it later that day, and by the next morning I had published my first issue to my three subscribers: Mike Hopkins at Mike Hopkins Distributing Co. in Brenham, Texas; Larry Del Papa at Del Papa Distributing in Galveston; and my father, who was retired and living in Santa Fe. Since that day, I have done nothing else for fifteen years.

So thank you for drinking beer. What follows here are stories and essays that shed light on both the beer industry and the special kind of trouble one might get into while covering it extensively.

H.S.

HITTING THE BRICKS

FOR A YEAR AND a half, we left our toddler son Hunt swaddled on a couch in a drafty hallway at my wife's family's equestrian camp — sucking his thumb and watching a small television with the Disney movie *The Aristocats* on a continuous loop. It was one of those little TVs that had a VHS tape player built into it, and one of the great features of this TV — no doubt to make up for the fact that it only had a 10-inch screen — was that it would play a video tape and then rewind the tape automatically and play it again. *The Aristocats* was an animated 1970s film typical of the Disney tradition of the time; it featured talking animals getting drunk and being mildly racist, among other things. In this case, the story followed a family of rich white cats, which, through the services of an ill-intentioned union butler, are dumped on the wrong side of town and get stuck with brown alley cats. But after encountering several intoxicated geese and a dog so drunk he can barely speak, the white cats eventually make their way back to the rich part of town with the help of a lighter brown alley cat. Order is restored.

Hunt loved *The Aristocats*. He loved it so much that he pretty much spent most of his time on the couch watching it. Not that he had much of a choice. My wife Lulu was supporting us by running her parents' equestrian camp on Lake Austin while I was trying to get *Beer Business Daily* off the ground. *The Aristocats*, and that tiny VHS television that could play it on a continuous loop, was essentially a cheap babysitter.

The Aristocats is just one little example of the types of sacrifices — or concessions, rather — one makes when one is trying to start a new business. After I quit my job at the beer distributorship in 1996 and attended school up north for a year, we ran out of money. I somehow forgot that when you quit a job, they quit paying you. It's an important distinction. Write that down as a pro-tip, Ethel.

And if you happen to be lucky enough to have a company car, they also expect you to give that back when you quit. So I had to buy a car. Not having much cash on hand, I opted for style on the cheap: a 1971 cherry-red Oldsmobile ragtop. It had a cassette tape of *Neil Diamond's Greatest Hits* stuck in the radio, and — like *The Aristocats* — it played on a continuous loop. To this day, when I see *The Aristocats* or hear Neil Diamond, it makes me feel ... poor. Oh, and the convertible top didn't close, so I'd have to throw a tarp over the car when it rained. The car also inexplicably honked every time you turned left, so the entire family got in the habit of waving every time we turned left so it didn't look like we were just being assholes.

Beer Business Daily had about 200 customers, about half of whom were regularly paying. It was not a rich living. The subscriber base was not growing. The news I was writing was sterile. And outside of Texas, I knew very few people in the industry. I was stuck and it didn't look like I was going anywhere. I worked as a consultant for a while, did some marketing work for local distributor (and good friend) John Gillis for a while, but now I was trying to make a real go of it. And so I found myself living at my in-laws' horse-and-waterskiing camp on Lake Austin off my wife's meager income as a camp director.

And Lulu got really busy running the camp. Their convention business took off when companies like Dell and Intel started hosting "off-sites" at the place regularly. It took so much of her time, in fact, that I found myself going days only seeing her from afar, usually in a bikini in the lake or on a horse. We would schedule weekly conjugal visits, but it was clear that our poverty was driving us apart.

I knew that I had to "hit the bricks," a figure of speech I had chosen to mean that I needed to get out there and actually meet people in the industry I was covering. There wasn't much of an internet at this point, so that meant traveling and working the phones. I decided I needed an office to have privacy and a dedicated phone, so I rented a tiny office in the nearby resort town of Lakeway.

My wife's younger brother Todd lived in a small house on the property as well, trying to make it as a commercial real estate broker. He worked off commissions, which meant he was just as broke as I was. Since starting my car was often a two-person affair — one person to turn the ignition and one person to spray flammable liquid into the carburetor — Todd was often my co-pilot on excursions into town.

When you're poor and depressed and there doesn't seem like there's much hope (and you can't afford cable TV), you look for things to occupy your mind. A role model, perhaps. For Todd and me, it was a man named Rockey Piazza.

Rockey Piazza was – is – a mover and shaker in Lakeway circles. His name adorned just about every real estate sign, he owned a hot Mexican food restaurant, he built strip centers, he owned those places where you store boats. He drove a giant black Hummer — not the GM model, but an actual converted Humvee. Rockey was our god. Todd and I made a game of who could get the most "Rockey sightings." If you saw him in his car, that was just one point, because he drove that monstrosity all over Lakeway seemingly all the time. You got two points if you saw him just out in public, outside the safety of the Humvee. If you actually spoke to him, well, that was a hundred points.

Todd: "I saw Rockey today at the grocery store."

Me (marveling and green with envy): "What was he wearing?"

Todd: "Black turtleneck, khaki slacks, and eel skin boots."

Me: "Did you talk to him?"

Todd: "I almost did, but he turned away at the last minute."

Me: "I thought I saw him at the bank yesterday, but then I remembered that his car doesn't fit in the drive-through lane, so it must've been someone else."

One day Todd and I were at a restaurant and Rockey Piazza was eating next to us. We got the nerve to walk up and introduce ourselves, as if he were some sort of celebrity, which he was. I was surprised to find that he had a higher-pitched voice than I expected. Success comes in many forms.

I used to think, *If I could just be as successful as Rockey Piazza, I will have made it*. I just needed to hit the bricks.

But hitting the bricks is harder than it would appear. Some days Todd would show up with a twelve pack of Lone Star Light and we'd sit in the creek and drink it. Some days we'd go into town seeing if we could spot Rockey Piazza. Some days we'd drive into Austin and hit the bars on Sixth Street. Some days we'd hang out at the Burger Hut, reading about rich people in *Forbes* magazine, because that's what we thought successful businessmen did (plus Burger Hut had a subscription so we could read it for free). This is when I'd feel at my lowest, because I felt like a failure and I could not imagine that I would ever be successful in a career that I loved. I had read about some thirty-year-old prick millionaire who had just invented a plastic that doesn't melt, and here I was eating at Burger Hut with my virtually unemployed younger brother-in-law and two young children, one of whom was attending school in a redneck district and developing a distinct country accent, while the other was learning warped class distinctions from Disney on an endless loop. I had been miserable working at the beer distributorship, but at least it paid the bills. I started thinking that maybe I had made a mistake.

Me: "I'm thinking of moving back to Houston and asking for my old job back."

Todd (absently flipping through a *Forbes*): "Don't move this week; you'll miss the season finale of *Ally McBeal*."

Yes, we watched *Ally McBeal* every Tuesday night at Todd's place. It was the highlight of our week. That's how low we'd fallen.

To make matters worse, Lulu and I weren't getting along. I resented the fact that she was working so hard and didn't have any time for me, and she resented me because she was having to work so hard to support us while I "dallied on my little newsletter."

I needed to hit the bricks. I summoned Lulu to Rockey Piazza's restaurant in Lakeway. We needed to talk, and it wasn't going to be pleasant. (For the record, Rockey was not there.)

Me: "I've been lonely and in need of someone. As though I'd done something wrong somewhere, but I don't know where, come lately."

Lulu (frowning at her frijoles): "Um, it sounds like you're just quoting a Neil Diamond song."

Me: "Lulu, let me ask you something: Have you ever read about a frog who dreamed of being a king …?"

Lulu (leaving): "You really need to get rid of that car."

Me: "I want to fly on the wings of a flea …"

Lulu: "Goodbye."

In the end, I decided to go back to Houston, hat in hand, and ask my old employer, Joe Huggins, for my old job back. But this was met with some resistance on the home front. Lulu leveled with me in the kitchen on the day of my departure.

"If you leave Austin, don't come back."

"Fine!" I said, and stormed out.

She made herself some coffee and sat down at the kitchen table. Five minutes later I darkened her door again.

"Uh, can you give me a jump? My car is dead."

Nothing like making a dramatic exit for effect and then having to come back to ask your nearly estranged wife to help you start your car.

My trip to Houston was not fruitful. I sat drinking with Joe Huggins all afternoon at his favorite watering hole, The Hofbrau. He spent nearly every afternoon there and they had installed a phone for him at his seat so he could conduct business. In the end, Joe said, "You were meant to be a writer, and if I give you back your job, you'll always regret it. I'm doing you a favor in sending you away. You need to hit the bricks."

I dawdled in Houston for two weeks, staying at my friend Jeff Smith's house. I didn't know what to do with myself. I was broke, I didn't know if I had a family, I didn't have a place to live. Jeff and his wife were generous hosts, but I couldn't stay in their guest bedroom forever. I thought of returning to San Antonio and selling odd-shaped rocks or carving wooden figurines out of cedar sticks and selling them on the Riverwalk.

Lulu and I had a wedding to attend in the Bahamas for good friends in a few days, and I didn't know if we were going as a couple or not. It turns out we flew to Harbour Island together but went our separate ways as soon as we hit the ground. We'd meet one another each night at our cabana, which was dubbed—inaccurately at the time—the "love shack." Later she and some friends totaled a golf cart by driving it into the ocean and presented me with the bill. I had to borrow money from my grandmother to pay it.

I needed to hit the bricks.

After the Bahamas, I returned to Austin and stayed at Todd's house. He was tactful enough not to ask too many questions about why I wasn't staying with his sister.

Todd: "So ... *Ally McBeal* tonight?"

Me: "You know it. I've missed a few episodes, so you'll have to catch me up." (This was pre-TiVo.)

I looked out the window and could see Lulu in her yellow bikini on the lake, driving the boat with a skier in tow. The water shimmered like tarnished silver. She was tan from the Bahamas, 29 years old with long legs, a blond ponytail whipping in the wind. It was a sight that takes your breath away. What I didn't know at that point was that she was pregnant with our third son. (Before you ask, yes, the boy is mine.)

Me: "I guess I need to patch things up with Roscoe." (That was our nickname for her for some reason.)

Todd: "Yep. And we both need to hit the bricks."

Todd was at a breaking point as well. He had not made a commission in ten months, and he owed the IRS money from his last commission.

Later I walked down to the main house to catch Lulu in the kitchen making a giant pot of beans for the campers. I told her that I missed her, and to my surprise, she burst into tears and said she missed me, too. I told her I was going to hit the bricks, for real this time, because there were no other choices left. She agreed.

~*~

There was one obstacle in our path: We had no money, and nobody thought *Beer Business Daily* would make it. Hell, *I* wasn't even sure it would make it. You know how in biographies people say things like, "Nobody believed my idea would work, but I knew my passion for such-and-such and hard work would carry the day." Well, I wasn't that guy. I mean, I *thought* it would work for reasons I'll get into, but I wasn't completely convinced. Look, I had read enough *Forbes* articles at the Burger Hut to know that no amount of passion and hard work can compensate for a shitty idea, and almost everybody thought *Beer Business Daily* was a shitty idea.

Let's count the reasons:

1. There was already a well-respected trade newsletter in the beer industry, *Beer Marketer's Insights*, where the editor, Benj Steinman, was beloved. He had a huge head start on sources and access.

2. Beer industry people don't have a lot of desk time to read. Industry people routinely told me, "We don't need another publication, especially not a *daily*. It's too much to read."

3. Most senior beer industry people — the people who could afford or had the authority to pay for such a publication — weren't using email back then.

4. There were no blogs and very few "for pay" news websites back then. So the idea of a daily electronic publication sent via email and on a paywalled website had to first be explained before I could even try to sell it. (Even when I was successful in selling a subscription, people would invariably give me their mailing address to send it.)

5. There are some days when there is just no news.

It may be hard to remember, but daily publishing was rare then, particularly for niche B2B trade publications covering a narrow industry. And the email/website publications were almost universally free. My idea to charge a few hundred dollars a year and deliver the news daily via email and a website with a paywall may not have been exactly revolutionary, but at the very least it was novel. The only publication that charged for content online back then was the *Wall Street Journal*, and in fact, I designed our first website after wsj.com.

People regularly told me that there wasn't enough beer news to publish every day. My father also pointed out that being tied to a daily publication was an inconvenience. "You've effectively chained yourself every day to a computer and internet connection."

That statement seems ludicrous today, as everybody is chained to their devices and connected to the net every minute of every day. But back then, it was quite difficult to get online. Wireless? A pipe dream. There was no wifi or cellular data. You had to dial in. Sometimes there was no local dial-in number, so you had to dial long distance and pay a fee by the minute. Traveling was difficult because there was no wifi in airports or on planes. For the first ten years or so of publishing BBD, I often had to research and write issues late at night after I had already traveled across the country all day and attended meetings. It was exhausting. So my father proved to be prescient.

There were many hectic days when I'd be banging my head against the wall, thinking, *Why didn't I call it Beer Business Every-Other-Day??*

Today, everybody publishes daily, sometimes several times a day. Many news sites are moving to a paywall for premium content. And connectivity is not a problem.

And while some might say that now anyone with a blog can create more competition for guys like me, who are charging a hefty price, I would say that this is an *opportunity* — an opportunity to stand out by adding context, opinions, and perhaps most unusual for a trade publication, humor. And being so digitally connected has vastly freed up where I can be and liberated me from my desk. It makes the job much more enjoyable.

~*~

After a brief consulting gig in Denver so I could pay for a baby being born, Lulu and I packed up our three kids and moved to San

Antonio, where I'm from. I borrowed $20k from my mother and $20k from my mother-in-law's boyfriend (now husband), movie director Terrence Malick, to buy me a year to make this bitch of a publication work or not. I also optioned a screenplay based on the life of William Tell. I would use $30k to live on and $10k to travel around the country to beer conventions and distributor meetings to meet people in the industry. I installed a window unit A/C and a card table in my garage and so created an office.

I devised a three-point plan:

1. I sent out a mailer to each state's beer distributor association executive (almost every state has a beer lobbyist, and that person also organizes each state's annual distributor confab) and basically told them I would speak at their annual meeting free of charge. About ten agreed right off the bat. Then another fifteen. Within the first year, I got Platinum status on American Airlines. I started meeting distributors and brewers in their home states, shook hands, got my name out there — yes, I made friends. And this wasn't easy for me, because I was actually quite shy and awkward at the time and had no experience giving speeches. But when you have an idea that you have to sell that most people have already told you is a

shitty idea, and you have three kids and a blond wife at home to feed, you pretty much just do what you have to fucking do.

It was during that time that I was attending a beer convention in New Orleans and was sitting at the bar with New Belgium Brewing's JB Shireman, who was running distributor relations. He later tells the story that he was concerned about me because it didn't appear I was making very much money. "Harry," he said, "is this thing going to work out?" And I apparently said, "Oh, yeah! I expect to be well into the four figures this year."

2. Next, I decided to abandon the sterile newspaper writing style and write in a manner that reflected my personality and offer commentary of what I really thought on an issue — and put some humor in the damn thing. Again, not exactly revolutionary today when you have sites like *Gawker* or even the *New York Observer*. But back then, it was journalistic sacrilege to insert your personality into a story. The *AP Stylebook* forbade it. Worse, it was a huge risk, because you would likely alienate many people with your salty commentary, particularly those who don't have a sense of humor.

But as soon as I started commenting on stories and peppering them with humor, readership increased immediately, and I noticed that open rates on emails soared. Our email open rate today is well over 100 percent, which means that for each issue of BBD sent out, it is opened more than once on average. Yes, some readers invariably get pissed off with the stances we take, but I've found that those that are the most pissed off send back their renewal checks the quickest. We have a motto around here: If you're not pissing off at least a quarter of your readers at any given time, you're not doing your job.

3. Third, when I wasn't traveling, I forced myself to cold call at least half a dozen wholesalers a day. This was grueling and unglamorous work, but it paid off because I would usually get a hold of one or two and — if not make a sale — we would at least get to know each other, which would generate a source for the future.

~*~

So I flew to Des Moines and Tumwater and Palm Beach, and I gave the speeches, and I shook the hands at beer receptions, and I handed out the business cards, and I offered the two month free trial subscriptions. And guess what? People started subscribing. As more people read, I got access to more sources and my content improved. People actually began sending me unsolicited tips. It was a virtuous cycle. Beer industry insiders started asking others, "Did you read Harry today?" I was on the path of making a living. And while I was perpetually exhausted as the sole editor, circulation administrator, bookkeeper, site developer, IT guy, et cetera, rolled into one, I was meeting great people, making new friends, and generally having a ball. More and more people recognized me at meetings and conventions, and instead of standing around with my thumb in my butt, folks were engaging me and including me into their conversations.

But the publication was still much smaller than the competition and lacked some credibility with some folks on account of its freewheeling editorial style. It's hard to take a news publication seriously when you're using words like, "bozo," and "fermentationally challenged."

A break of sorts came about when South African Breweries purchased Miller Brewing Company. On a hunch, I had stayed up late and so was the first to report that story, and within months their newly bought and largest division was being run by a newcomer from South Africa: Norman

Adami. A no-nonsense guy, Adami immediately fixated on a strategy called the "able challenger," meaning they would fight their much larger competitor, Anheuser-Busch, not on Anheuser-Busch's terms, but on Miller's terms. That meant poking A-B at every turn, including in media relations, which is where I came in.

When Adami came onto the scene, I had a decent relationship with Miller Brewing, an okay relationship with Coors Brewing Co., and no relationship at all with Anheuser-Busch; meanwhile, my competition enjoyed unfettered relationships with all three, especially A-B. Norman saw an opportunity there and decided to give me, the tiny publication with limited access to the big three brewers, a break. He not only returned my calls on stories, he actively called me with exclusives. Being on the crest of breaking news from the second-largest brewery in the country provided added credibility to BBD and a good dose of content.

But the most important meeting of the year — the big kahuna — was the Beer Institute meeting. Not because of its size (the National Beer Wholesalers annual convention is much larger), but because it's so exclusive that only a couple hundred people attend each year, and it's the right people. If you want to build relationships with the top people in the beer industry, the Beer Institute annual meeting was the place to do it. But I could not get an invitation to attend while my competitors did. The president of the Beer Institute at the time, the late Jeff Becker, called me and said, "Listen pal, you didn't get the bid again this year, but I'm pulling for you." I asked him why, and he evaded my question.

Later I learned why.

As I said, my relationship at the time with A-B was non-existent and, in at least one instance, hostile. In one article, I referred to August Busch IV, who had a reputation as a playboy and was prone to scandal, as "the Ted Kennedy of the beer business." This article was passed around and fell into the hands of August IV's father, August Busch III, who became infuriated and allegedly black-balled me from the meeting, according to friends who were on the board at the time. But eventually Norman Adami ascended to the board and invited me to attend. I've been going ever since.

Ironically, while my little joke about August Busch IV is what got me banned, it was August Busch IV himself with whom I eventually forged a relationship and who thus got me access to Anheuser-Busch. And I would say we ended up being friends of a sort for a time.

And finally, the last piece of the puzzle of my "hitting the bricks" plan: I decided I needed to host some sort of annual seminar with top industry executives to gain more credibility for my little publication. Actually, a southern beer distributor, Paul Bertucci, first put the bug in my ear while we were eating oysters in Gulfport, Mississippi.

"You ought do it, man. I know it's a big risk with renting out the hotel and such, but you just need to man-up and pull the trigger and quit being a pussy." (Bertucci is a king when it comes to figures of speech, in case you couldn't tell.) He then added, "I'd pay to go to it; you know that." It was a good idea, but he didn't attend the first one. I tease him to this day, but he's been to all the others.

We held the first Beer Industry Summit in Richmond, Virginia, at the Jefferson Hotel — in July. Why Richmond in July, when it was 100 degrees and as humid as a dog's mouth? Well, my mother-in-law had recently married the movie director and writer Terrence Malick, a benefactor of BBD's, and Terrence was shooting a movie called *A New World* in the woods near

Richmond. My wife packed up the kids for the summer and moved to studio lodging to loiter on the set each day so she could hang out with Colin Farrell, I suppose. Not wanting to leave my wife on a set alone with Colin Farrell, I decided to accompany her. And besides, my favorite actor, Christopher Plummer, was also on the set. So I decided to have that first Beer Summit in Richmond because I was essentially living there at the time. We were able to get only one C-level executive at any of the major breweries to show up and speak. And yes, it was Norman Adami. About ninety people attended, which made it barely break even, but news spread that the event was entertaining and (!!!) even provided some valuable information.

The next year, we had it in Chicago in January. Another brilliant climate move. On the suggestion cards we handed out at the end of the summit, people helpfully suggested that we not hold next year's event in a place with horizontal snow. But we were able to swing not only Norman Adami again, but the new CEO of Anheuser-Busch, August Busch IV. Just before August was scheduled to speak, we got word that his Learjet was circling overhead looking for a window in the blizzard to land. I was able to move speaker slots around, stall, and generally sweat it out until he finally strolled into the meeting hall at the last minute, followed by his entourage. Without missing a beat, he walked right up to the podium and began speaking.

I had learned my lesson — the Beer Summit was to be held in reasonable climates from then on. We still hold it in the winter, but it's in places like San Diego, Miami, and Scottsdale. And we get over four hundred participants these days. The Summit proved to be not only a nice profit center for our company, but more importantly, it has morphed into the event that top execs feel compelled to attend each year. It's the ideal forum where things get done in the U.S. beer industry.

Eventually I paid back Terrence and my mother the money they lent me, but I was still a one-and-a-half man operation. The half was a young intern named Tiffani (she dotted the second "i" with a heart) to help out with renewals whenever she bothered to show up. (In the end, I actually had trouble tracking her down to fire her.) But I knew that I needed help, not just with administrative work, but with editing the newsletter and preparing for each year's

Beer Summit. I couldn't do it all and still expect to live past 40.

As many of you know, it's crucial to a small company to get your first real hire right — right in that person's work ethic, compatibility in working with you, intelligence, personality, and drive. And in my case, I wanted this person to live in San Antonio — not exactly a mecca in journalism circles. If you get the wrong person, it can be very costly in money and time, and those were two commodities we didn't have in abundance at BBD. If I got this decision wrong, I could go broke.

I put an ad on Monster.com and got back about a hundred resumes. After work, I would sift through them, but the vast majority were unqualified or lived in Toronto or were just job trolls. I was getting very frustrated.

Then one night while lying in bed and going through resumes, I found one that sounded moderately promising: a recent English Lit grad from TCU. I was hoping for journalism, but her clips weren't bad and she seemed motivated to get a writing job in Texas. Besides, hers was the only resume I got that offered even the remotest qualifications. At the time, she was driving through the Rockies with some friends that summer before beginning her working life. We set a time and I called her on her cell phone. Reception was spotty, but I got enough from our conversation to ascertain that she was sane, and even bright, although I swore I heard somebody in the back seat say "Pass the joint." No matter, after a series of interviews, I knew that this was the right person.

Megan Haverkorn was fresh out of college, eager to learn, and most of all didn't want to be a teacher, which she thought would be her fallback position if she couldn't find an editing job. She was professional, attractive, and very well put-together for a girl from Longview, Texas. I hired her on the spot after our first in-person interview, then dragged her to Las Vegas almost immediately for the wholesale beer convention. She later claimed that I never budgeted time to eat, sleep, or even go to the bathroom for three days. Welcome to working for a small company in the beer business.

The long and short of it is that I hired the right person in Megan. It hasn't all been roses — she has spoken to me at decibels and in tones that would curl the toes of a cage fighter (I'm not a very consistent or effective manager sometimes, it seems). But nobody has done more to help me grow this company than Megan, and she provided the catalyst that moved the company from a one-man show in dire straits to a real company.

I had finally hit the bricks, and it paid off. *Beer Business Daily* became a ten-year overnight success.

A Conversation With My Dog

My two sisters and I own a ranch near Leon Springs, Texas. It's been in the family for three generations and I grew up there. The house is situated on a wide tract of rocky, uneven terrain dotted with watering holes and covered with scrubby grass and bushes teeming with flies, chiggers, and snakes. The land sustains some cattle, deer, donkeys, and a zebra or two. Occasionally a zebra and a donkey will go at it and we wind up getting zedonks running around the property. It's like the Island of Dr. Moreau.

The house itself is sprawling — it was built in the late 1940s when it was considered gauche to have a second story, so you just built wing upon wing. I can't promise you the house would fit in a regulation rugby field. The newspaper business was good to granddad and his father, who were the publishers of the *San Antonio Express* — this was back when newspapers were profitable.

Like I said, early in my marriage my rib Lulu and I found ourselves with two little children and completely broke. I was between jobs (which is a euphemism for unemployable) and so we moved out to the ranch temporarily to avoid rents and mortgages. It's funny how temporary is in the eye of the beholder, you see. In my mind's eye, temporary could mean five years. In my sisters' eyes, maybe a month? After about six months my sister Diana finally called in her frank way and said, "Hey, you ever moving out of the ranch and maybe, I don't know, getting a job?"

"You're never even here. I could tell you I already moved out and you'd never know," I said.

"So have you, then?"

"Well…. No."

The problem was I really didn't want to leave. At the time I envisioned a sort of Henry David Thoreau existence, where I would sell odd-shaped rocks at the farmer's market for cash and eat rabbits and such. The chink in the armor was my wife did not share this vision of Utopia. Between my sisters, my wife, and my mother (who also tended to chime in from time to time on my relative vagabondery), pressure finally brought my year of lethargic self-reflection to an end, and I started *Beer Business Daily* to generate income so my family would stop despising me.

Eventually *BBD* became profitable and we bought a house in the Alamo Heights region of San Antonio, where you could walk outside and see people and houses instead of cows and zedonks. To take the edge off not being immersed in nature we bought a dog named Chica. She's dead now (I think — she's definitely gone) but while she was alive and around, she was great for giving advice.

Friday nights were devoted to dinners with our friends at a Mexican joint here in San Antonio called Paloma Blanca. Now, Paloma has this lethal margarita called The Heights. It's more like a martini with tequila substituted for the gin and lime juice substituted for the vermouth. There's a saying around here about The Heights margarita: They're like boobs — one is not enough, two is good, three ain't right, and four is perfect. So naturally, I would have four. After that, Lulu would take me home and I would get in the hot tub, as is my wont. And usually, Chica would join me.

I long ago discovered that four Heights margaritas have the surprising benefit of endowing one with the temporary ability to speak and understand dog. So one night, after four rounds of Heights margaritas, Chica walked straight up to the hot tub and said in her English Wapping waterfront accent, "Excuse me, guv'nor, may I join you?"

As a puppy Chica was taught to have the best manners, for although she's hackney and a dog, she could easily sit at the Queen's table without dishonor. She stepped into the tub and took her usual seat in the corner with the strongest jet.

Chica, being a dog, is naturally stupid in comparison to humans. She can't count, has no self-awareness and can't drive a golf cart, despite repeated attempts to teach her. But unlike most humans, she is not unwise. She knows instinctively that meat is always preferable to fruit and vegetables, and that if you see an unattended cake on the counter, go ahead and hop up there and eat the entire thing immediately, because you never know when you'll run across another unattended cake.

Chica is also a practiced aficionado of pork and venison sausage, and she knows that the best ratio of pork to venison is 60-

40. She also loves, and I mean *loves*, to run in front of the golf cart at the ranch. She can run for hours. In fact, if you don't stop her, she'll run herself to death. So although she eats lots of sausage and cake, she stays trim by running in front of the buggy. That and chasing the two neighborhood cats, Gary and Tiger, who make a daily game of taunting her.

I lit a cigar and settled in.

"Chica," I said, blowing smoke in her face. She likes it. Secondhand smoke is the only way she gets to enjoy a good cigar, lacking opposable thumbs like a raccoon, or even fingers. At least raccoons have fingers and can conceivably smoke cigars, although they'd have a hell of a time lighting one. "Chica, what is the meaning of life?"

"Sausage of course, guv'nor," said she.

"Have you ever seen how sausage is made?"

"Does it really matter, guv'nor?"

I contemplated this as I took another puff. "Good point," I murmured. Like I said, Chica is so wise. "Chica, I get so many emails these days, I am having trouble getting to them all in a timely manner; and worse, I am overlooking important emails that sometimes never get returned. What should I do?"

Chica ponders this for a minute. "Sometimes," said she, "late in the autumn when we have exhausted our sausage supply, our lady Lulu will give me a rawhide bone instead. It's a poor substitute, but dogs cannot be choosers …"

"Is this going anywhere, Chica?"

"Stay with me here, guv'nor. Every now and then she forgets that she has given me a rawhide bone, and she will give me another …"

"She never forgets when she throws me a bone, Chica, eh?" I interjected.

"Please let me finish," Chica said with some irritation. Some dogs have no sense of humor. Her blood sugar must have been low. "So then I have two bones. I can't chew on both bones at the same time, unfortunately. And I can't leave a bone lying around, lest one of those slutty mouse-eating, mange-ridden tabbies get hold of it. So I bury one bone — the bone that is the lesser of the two bones — and I chew on the better bone until such time that it is properly consumed. Always eat the good bone first, as you never know when you'll get run over by the mailman. Then I go and dig up the other one. That is the solution to your email problem."

I chew on this for a while. Yes, I can prioritize my emails, return the ones needing immediate attention, and then carve out time in the evening or weekend to return the other emails that have been saved off. Brilliant!

"You are very wise, Chica. Another question: Why are we bailing out the losing industries in our economy and taxing the successful ones?"

"Everybody loves the underdog," said she with a sigh. Or was that gas? Then after a pause: "Look, guv'nor, I have to ask before the Heights margaritas wear off — will you tell Lulu that I prefer the cheap generic dog food from HEB, not that expensive Science Diet. It gives me gas." Ah, so that's what it was. "Also, tomorrow after the lad's baseball practice, can we go to the ranch so I can run in front of the buggy?"

"Yes," I said. "We shall spend many hours in the buggy tomorrow, after I return my emails." And then, just as quick as that, her hackney waterfront accent returned to a regular Labrador bark. I patted her on the head and we silently enjoyed the rest of our cigar together.

THE BEER-DRINKING GOAT

SO IT WAS MY birthday, sweet forty-four and never been kissed. I become intolerable anywhere near my birthday. Even during "normal" times of the year I can be obnoxious, but during my birthday I insist that it be the All About Harry Show, starring ... Harry.

Quite naturally, this means that I don't have many friends. So be it. Friends are for losers. And they get in the way of quality beer journalism, and they sometimes want to blather on about their tedious domestic problems. Who needs that?

Not me. And besides, I don't need friends; I have Lulu, and she has friends I can rent. So for my forty-fourth birthday, Lulu gave me a birthday party and invited all her friends, plus one of my few friends, Christy, whom I keep as a friend only because she's low-maintenance and doesn't have any problems. Christy also happens to own a cafe and thus catered the party. So I guess she would have been there regardless. But I digress.

The party was, by most accounts, a blowout, except that I have yet to fulfill a long-standing birthday wish. You see, for many a moon my only desire on my birthday is to rent a karaoke machine so that I can sing ballads to (not *with*) Lulu's friends as I sit on a throne on a stage and wear a crown on my head. I would hold a microphone in one hand ("This one goes out to all the girls I've loved before…"), and a gold scepter in the other.

Guests would be regaled with such classics, belted out in my best baritone, as "How Do You Like Me Now!" and "I Like Your Bedonkadonk" and "The Lady Is a Tramp," as I point to various of Lulu's pretty friends with my scepter. Lulu, who is wise in not only how to make friends, but keep them, draws the line, and I have yet to play rock star on my birthday, even though it is *my* birthday, not hers. If she wants to dance on a coffee table and take her top off at her birthday, far be it from me to stop her. But that's the kind of double standard I live with every day, folks.

You know something that really chaps my mash tun? It can be your birthday, and some schmuck comes up to you and says something like, "Yeah it was my birthday last week," or worse, "My birthday is tomorrow, you know." Well you know what? I could give a flying monkey when your birthday is, because it's my birthday and my birthday party. You see who's wearing the crown, pal? You see this scepter?? *Do you see this golden scepter?!* I got some bad news for you, buddy — choo-choo! Here comes the clue train, and you're about to get hit. Right before your birthday.

To balance out this borderline hedonism, I also took my two oldest sons, Harrison and Hunt, on a trip to probably one of the most overlooked destinations for families who enjoy and appreciate beer: Lajitas.

We decided to forego the usual tourist traps, mainly because I don't cotton to being around a bunch of strangers' children, or waiting in long lines, or really any crowds at all. Therefore, we spent a glorious week in beautiful Lajitas along the far west Texas-Mexican border. No crowds there. No people at all, really. Just a goat. It was bliss.

Lajitas is a one-goat town, and this goat is also the mayor and he drinks Lone Star beer. I'll take some time so you can read that sentence again.

Welcome back.

This goat, Clay Henry III, is not even the first goat to be mayor of Lajitas. That distinction goes to his grandfather, Clay Henry I, who also was a fan of Lone Star beer, as was Clay Henry, Jr.

The New York Times reported in 2002 that Clay Henry III "is not a strategic planner," which is probably the understatement of the decade. (The *Times* reporter, Jim Yardley, also noted the following about Lajitas: "This isolated place along the Rio Grande is called the end of the road, but it might as well be the end of the world.")

Despite a perceived lack of strategic planning, Clay Henry III handily won the 2000 election for Lajitas mayor against a formidable field of worthy candidates that included a wooden Indian and a dog named Clyde.

When a town has an actual goat as the official mayor, and the goat likes beer — well, you either need to admire that or just shake your head in disgust. I chose to admire it because you can't change what you can't change.

When I mentioned my birthday vacation in *Beer Business Daily*, Jim Koch, the co-founder and chairman of the Boston Beer Company, emailed me with a query.

"Why on earth, with all the subscriptions (expensive subscriptions) Boston Beer Co. has, would you take your kids to Lajitas?" he wrote.

Jim had worked near there in the 1970s and knew its charms, or lack thereof. My boys asked the same question, quite vociferously and often throughout the trip.

"Look," I told them, "there are starving children in Africa who don't get to slide down bentonite hills on their bottoms, feed beer to, and catch fleas from, a goat that is also a public official; ingest a dysentery-causing amoeba in Mexico; hit golf balls over the Rio Grande and have illegals bring them back to you; and fall hands-first into cacti." I paused to take a pull from a Lone Star while they sulked. "So count your blessings you spoiled little brats."

My oldest son, when asked later by a friend where he went for vacation, replied, "Uh, we went to the desert and saw a lot of rocks."

Okay, I get it. Lajitas and the side trips to Terlingua and Marathon and Marfa aren't exactly Disneyland, but doggonit, Disneyland isn't real. It's a company that creates this false environment with annoying music and hordes of people everywhere, any number of whom may be carriers of some variety of animal-prefixed flu — bird, swine, bovine ... do you really want to risk getting bovine influenza from standing in a mile-long line for "It's a Small World"? Think about it.

The rocks in Lajitas are real and don't carry viruses, and the Montezuma's Revenge we caught at Ma Crosby's in Acuna was certainly real, and it held the benefit of being a great start to losing weight at the beginning of the New Year, when all the other poor saps were trying to do it in a gym with some half-hearted resolution.

This trip was actually a family-heritage homecoming for this beer journalist. This very border town was the secret spot where a young cub reporter with San Antonio's daily newspaper of record was able to secure the interview of a lifetime. It was the no-man's land of journalistic time periods just after WWI but before WWII. At the time, the interview was the journalistic coup of the decade, and subsequent interviews were syndicated to newspapers via telegraph across the land and made the young newsman a minor celebrity. The exclusive interviews, held in Lajitas over a two-year period, were with renegade Mexican revolutionary Francisco "Pancho" Villa, who was then on the lam since he was crossing the border and marauding American ranchers, so these meetings were in secret.

Harrison and Hunt listened, disinterested, as we sat at a bar called The Thirsty Goat. (They let children sit in bars in Lajitas; who's going to stop us, the mayor? He was passed out under a mesquite bush.)

The man who got the interviews, got the assignment mainly because he spoke Spanish and had roughly the same first name, so the editors felt he would be less likely to be shot by the insane bandit because the two had so much in common.

"And that man's name," I said with theatrical flair, "was Frank."

My middle boy, Hunt, then said sweetly, "My name is Frank."[1]

"Aye," I said wisely, drawing out the suspense — suspense holds a high value in the desert. "Both men were named Frank as you are, my young son. And the newspaperman named Frank of whom I speak was not shot. Frank, rather, forged a relationship with the renegade. And the newspaperman named Frank is …" — dramatic pause for effect — "… your great-grandfather."

It was like Darth Vader revealing his paternity to Luke.

And then to add cherries to the ice cream, I revealed how Frank parlayed that fleeting bit of fame, initiated arbitrarily by something as mundane as his first name, into eventually buying that newspaper and later serving as a U.S. Special envoy to Mexico, where he met his future wife.

"And that, my boys, is why you don't have to lather on sunscreen like a greased pig every single day like your pale, blond, Dutch mother," I said to them, then continued in a deep voice: "There are lessons to be learned here amongst these red rocks and goat, my boys: one, dark skin is better than light skin if you like to be outdoors a lot, and two, success is often started by dumb luck, so play the hand that's dealt you and play it hard."

I leaned back in my chair and crossed my arms with satisfaction, proud that I am able to convey such heavy universal truths to my three boys in a bar called The Thirsty Goat on my birthday. This got the boys interested for about a nano-minute.

"Wow. Cool story, Dad," Harrison said.

"Yeah," said Hunt, as he started biting a hangnail. Harrison looked at the exit then looked back at me.

"Can we slide down the hill on our butts again?"

Soon we were back to sliding down bentonite hills on our bottoms and trying to spin out on our golf cart and offering Lone Star to the mayor, who was now revived and happily munching on a thorny mesquite bush. Frank would have been proud, no?

---

[1] Frank is in fact his first name, but we call him by a shortened version of his middle name, Huntress. And yes, I know it sounds feminine, but it's a family name.

BEER MAN IN BEVERLY HILLS

I RECENTLY FOUND MYSELF in Los Angeles for a meeting. More specifically, I found myself in Beverly Hills (the wifi password for my hotel was "90210"). As a native Texan and beer man, I tend to be ill-equipped for the likes of Tinseltown, but I was lucky — at first.

The first night I was free, so I spent the evening catching up with some friends. As you know, I prefer my friends to be beautiful, smart, and funny. Or at least two out of three (that's why I hang out with beer people). I have three great friends in LA who possess all three traits in spades. One is a beautiful movie producer who worked on several great films you've heard of, one is a beautiful and brilliant young dermatologist who is one of the funniest gals I've ever met, and one is a software executive who lives in Beverly Hills and knows all the right spots.

We ended up at a hip bar in a small brick building that features a burlesque show set to a jazz band called 40 Deuce. The bar was basically a retro-speakeasy. We had to get past a doorman whose sole responsibility was to decide if the people who've made this little bar their chosen destination for the evening are worthy to enter. Perspiration sprouted on my forehead as we approached. Everybody I was with was very smartly dressed with one obvious exception.

"Are y'all sure I can get into this place?" I asked.

My navy blue blazer was a little wrinkled and missing some buttons (I rode a mechanical bull in it at a Pabst's party at the NBWA convention and some buttons were shorn off). And my shirt was a little frayed, and my scuffed New Balance sneakers were apparently not very fashion forward, as this hulking figure holding a clipboard, all six-feet-five-inches of him squeezed into a three-piece suit, frowned at my shoes long enough to make me jam my hands in my pockets and start slowly backing away. Luckily, my friends more than cancelled me out, and Mr. Frumpy was allowed in the door.

The place was small and very crowded. Everybody young, upscale, good-looking. Everything very retro, very 1920s, very loud. Since I didn't get out much outside of Leon Springs, Texas, I took notice of what they were drinking. Pear and peach martinis were everywhere. A few apple martinis. Lots of vodka cran and vodka red bull. A few rum and cokes. I drank my first and last mojito. I looked in vain for beer drinkers and finally found a couple drinking Coronas with lime. That was it. Just two out of probably 150 people. Very depressing. The Coronas, by the way, were five dollars and the martinis were eleven.

But my mood improved when I thought I spotted Catherine Zeta dash Jones. I don't normally get starry-eyed over actors, but Catherine Zeta dash Jones makes my knees weak. She sauntered over directly to me, looked me dead in the eyes, and said in a husky voice, "Is that the bathroom?"

I said, "Aye."

Get it? She's Irish. Or maybe she's Welsh. Doesn't matter, the joke works both ways, but apparently it was lost on Catherine Zeta dash Jones because she gave me a look as if I were wearing a meat helmet. Then my friend told me that not only was that not Catherine Zeta dash Jones, but it didn't even look like Catherine Zeta dash Jones other than the fact she had brown hair and was pretty. This is the second time I've misidentified a famous person. The first time was when I mistook my son's history teacher for Mr. Roper from *Three's Company*.

On my last day in Beverly Hills, I left the relative safety of my hotel room and wandered the streets for a few hours … down Rodeo Drive, around the corner to Wilshire, past the Creative Artists Agency — where I paused momentarily on the off chance I would spot the real Catherine Zeta dash Jones to see if I could woo her away from that wrinkled grandpa Michael Douglas — onto Santa Monica Boulevard, and back around to Beverly Hills Boulevard, just to look at all the fancy shiny things I can't afford since I have children who are so selfish as to want to go to college.

Two observations about Beverly Hills: The first is that isn't Beverly Hills supposed to be full of beautiful women? Most of the women I saw looked burned up and burned out, plastic orange skin, frizzed up hair, needlessly high heels, painted up like left bank French hookers, frozen pissed-off scowls on their vapid faces — probably have sand in their virginias. Several times I had to remind myself that I wasn't in the trashier parts of the red light district in Amsterdam (not that I've ever frequented the trashier parts of the red light district in Amsterdam … much). And many, like more than half (and all if over fifty) had those puffed up lips, where I guess a doctor shoots jello into them. What the hell is up with that? Does anybody suppose that this is desirable? They look like Audrey, the Venus flytrap in *Little Shop of Horrors*. Feed me, Seymour! This is the one time where jello isn't fun. They look like they were stung by hornets. My dear Catherine Zeta dash Jones would NEVER engage in this practice, though her vain octogenarian husband might. Moral of the story: If you want to look at pretty women who don't look like Yoda on Botox, don't waste your time in Beverly Hills. Austin has it beat twenty to one. And they smile at you. Hell, the girls trolling the Jersey Shore boardwalk are better than this.

The second observation is that the problem with Beverly Hills, or really any posh place, is that you can't purchase any essential toiletries. I needed a razor (the one I brought with me had about six weeks' use on it, so I think when I scraped it across my face hair actually sprouted), some chapstick (because I kept reflexively licking my lips when I saw all those artificially inflated pouts), and a legal pad, because I wanted to find a nice pub and work out next year's financial and marketing plan (because that's the kind of guy I am, productive even on a Saturday afternoon. Work, work, work). These seemingly mundane and ubiquitous items, which in most of America you can find on any given street corner, are simply not to be had in Beverly Hills. The reason, I suspect, is that rents are so high that a Rite-Aid would have to charge $5,000 for a small bottle of Pepto Bismol to make it on Rodeo Drive. Curious that in an area where you can buy a Cart-yee-air watch, a Louie Weetone suitcase, and an Alfalfa Romeo convertible, all within a 300-foot stretch of sidewalk, toothpaste is out of the question — at any price. So I went without. Such is sacrifice.

And forget about finding a nice neighborhood pub. The closest I could find was a fancy Italian restaurant that had a bar that seated two, because in Beverly Hills nobody drinks anything, except green drinks and cappuccinos — it's the only liquid that can pass those gigantic balloon lips apparently. Peroni Nasty As Euro was twelve dollars for a twelve-ounce "pint" (only in Beverly Hills would they recalibrate a standard unit of measure that's been in existence for well over two hundred years). I like Peroni, but this was testing the limits of my love for the Italian nectar.

But beggars can't be choosers, particularly when one is a beggar on Rodeo Drive. So I did my financial and marketing plan on a cocktail napkin with a borrowed Bic pen from the waitress, using my cell phone's calculator function to get the most out of the assets I already own. The waitress, incidentally, had poofy lips — twenty percent tips on twelve-dollar Peroni lets her live the High Life, no doubt. Where's Wendell when you need him? (These are insider beer industry jokes; my apologies to my friends who aren't in the industry. See, SABMiller owns Peroni and High Life, and there's this guy named Wendell that peddles High Life, and … well just rest assured, it's funny). As luck would have it, with the financial crisis, a napkin is all I needed, and I only needed one side. After I was done, I walked out into the sunlight, shading my eyes, stuffing my business plan (napkin) into the pocket of my fraying shirt, and there was a Bentley with the vanity license plates proclaiming "PRDUCER".

I hate this place, I thought.

~*~

Back in my hotel room, to add to my growing exasperation, I got an alarming email. At that time, my friend Kenneth and I both had six-year-old sons, and over cake and punch at one of their birthday parties, he approached me with an idea.

"How much fun would it be," Kenneth said, "to coach the boys' basketball team together this year?"

I indicated that I most certainly would not find it anywhere close to fun.

"I dislike basketball and I dislike children — at least other people's children — and I understand it takes a village, or more than two, to make a basketball team," I said. "So count me out."

But he needled and wheedled and said it would be a hoot and I wouldn't have to do much but occasionally show up to practices. After all, I'd only be the assistant coach. Finally I acquiesced just so my son couldn't claim in therapy after he grows up that I never coached any of his teams. Better to do it while they're still little and cute. Plus, I'd get to blow a whistle.

So you can imagine my surprise when I returned to my hotel room to a broadcast email from Karel, Kenneth's wife. Here is what it read:

Hi everyone! Here is our roster for the boys' basketball team. Harry Schuhmacher has agreed to be the head coach. Please let me know of any additional information you may need.
Thanks!
Karel on behalf of Harry Schuhmacher

Whaa? I didn't remember agreeing to being head coach. I thought we had agreed that KENNETH was to be head coach and I was to be a sort of belligerent Coach Friday standing off in the corner, blowing my whistle and occasionally slamming a yardstick on the bleachers to frighten the louder children. And is it me, or is her email a little overly chipper, in a mocking sort of way, with all its happy little exclamation points?

Now, Karel is cool and pretty and a good friend, so I sent her back an eloquently written and subtle email to get my point across, as one friend to another, while also attempting to catch a tone that contradicted her mocking chipper tone:

KAREL, WHAT THE FUCK?! -H

Satisfied that my meaning, however subtle, would be clear to her, I popped open a cold Heineken and turned on CNN.

Then I started thinking. You know, I've never liked the way the other dads who coach kids teams make it so serious and practices so boring and military-like, with their stupid soul-less, humorless, wicked fat faces incessantly shouting from the sidelines, "Billy get back there! Charlie move over there! Wyatt, stop scratching your butt!!" (That last one's my boy, and I resent it when some fat-face tells my little brilliant baby bear that he can't scratch what is evidently a chronic itch.) I've never said anything about it, because I'm firmly of the belief that you really can't register a complaint if you're not willing to step up to the plate yourself.

I popped a second Heineken. Maybe, just maybe, there is a better way. Maybe instead making every drill a chore, every game a shouting match, every season a relief that it's over, we can change the way it's done. Maybe we make each drill a little game. Maybe we dole out candy and trinkets as prizes for each drill. Maybe we create funny nicknames for each player. Maybe we pepper the practices intermittently with fart jokes — because six-year-olds can never resist a well-rendered fart joke. Maybe we create a secret unspoken code, like professional baseball players do, so there's zero noise from the sidelines. Maybe the players can scratch their butts freely without being harassed by fat-faced dads.

Maybe my revolutionary new coaching tactics work, and we actually win the championship and all the glory of this falls squarely where it should, on the shoulders of their head coach, whom they come to idolize. Maybe one of the players — maybe even my own boy — eventually becomes fabulously wealthy and famous and tells a black-tie crowd at some prestigious awards ceremony that he owes it all to his Kindergarten basketball coach, "my loving father, Harry Schuhmacher, who taught discipline and competitiveness" … or whatever basketball is supposed to teach you. I'll of course be long dead by this point, sitting on a mantle of clouds next to George Gervin, the legendary San Antonio Spur, the ICEMAN:

ICEMAN: "So which one's your boy?"

Me: "The one giving the speech."

ICEMAN: "The one scratching his butt?"

Me: "Yeah, that's my boy."

ICEMAN (inching away): "You must be proud …"

So, I popped one more Heineken, excited about my new endeavor, and penned the following email to Karel:

Dear Karel,

Upon reflection I have come to the conclusion that I don't wish to deny those boys the absolute best coach they can have, nor my son an education in discipline and competitiveness, so I agree to serve as head coach, with a few conditions.

First, will you please Google and print out the rules of basketball and some basketball drills that six year olds can do. Second, instruct Lulu to please go to Wal-Mart and buy me some cool sweat pants, blue, with the cool stripe down the sides, a cool matching jacket, with matching stripes down the arms, a loud-ass whistle, a loud-ass megaphone that can also play military marching songs, assorted candy (hard), assorted trinkets, a yardstick (just in case), some red cones (not sure why, but I think you're supposed to have red cones), a George Gervin poster, a case of Heineken, a propane tank, and one (1) glazed donut.

Those are my terms.
Yours,
Coach Schuhmacher

I added the donut just as a demonstration that Coach Schuhmacher's decisions will not be questioned.

~*~

Three Heinekens and a re-calibrated attitude about the future had me feeling optimistic. The future was looking bright. I could do this! Coach Schuhmacher could do this! I hopped out of bed and switched on the taps in the room's oversized tub to celebrate my newly acquired leadership with a bubble bath.

(Side note: Yes, I occasionally take bubble baths, particularly in hotel rooms. Some of my friends have suggested that taking bubble baths is not what men do. But I think au contraire. A fine hot bath with a scented candle and my favorite magazine ... okay, whatever, it's gay. Accept me like I am or don't, but I've loved taking baths since I was five years old. I had a Jacuzzi installed at home, which is just a bath outdoors.)

Turns out that day was not a good day for a bath. I drained the water and was stepping out, rather carelessly as I thought of the week's gripping events in the beer industry, and my right foot slipped out from under me. Gravity, in all its Newtonian glory, kicked in. Hard.

Now, there were four possible directions to fall:

1. I could have fallen back into the bathtub, in which case I would have braced myself against the walls,

2. I could have fallen toward the nice pile of soft pillowing towels ahead of me,

3. I could have fallen into the doorway where there was a fluffy carpet,
or,
4. I could have fallen left into a hard, cold, germ-laden, piss-stained, toilet.

Naturally, the toilet is where I fell. All 200-and-a-few-more pounds of me. And I didn't just hit the toilet, but I also struck the side of the tub somehow with a tremendous force, gravity having been extra strong that day, chest-first. There I was, with one hand in the bathtub, one hand in the toilet, my face in the space betwixt. I pushed myself like a fat oil-slathered seal onto the floor and started to sob hysterically like a little girl, holding my ribs and hip like some old woman. This, I declare, was not my finest hour. Those "I've fallen and I can't get up" beepers wouldn't have been any good to me, because I was stark naked, and I would rather lie there and die of internal injuries and hunger than let anybody see me like that, alive. Eventually, of course, they would find me, after rigor mortis had set in and presumably I would be decayed and drained of fluids a bit, (there was a "Do Not Disturb" sign on my door), likely making me look a little better than I did then.

I imagined Lulu receiving condolence calls from our friends. "Yes, it's such a tragedy, thank you for calling." Then in a flatter tone, "Yes, he really did fall into the toilet." I pictured our pastor at my funeral, grasping for nice things to say about me. "He was clumsy in life, but, uh, I'm sure God probably loves him." I imagined all my so-called guy friends coming a'calling around Lulu, trying to "give her comfort." Lulu, if you ever hear anybody say, "Harry would have wanted us to," don't believe them. I never want you to, again, ever. Never. Remember this: I'm either watching from above or below, but either way, I'm watching.

This last thought gave me strength. Must. Not. Die. Like. This. For good measure, I reached up and flushed the toilet. Couldn't see what's in it, but just in case. Like a true survivalist, I took stock of my situation, and tried to channel my inner Bear Grylls.

Keep your head on, Schuhmacher. Don't panic. You can get through this.

I felt around my body for broken bones. Tough to tell, a few places really, really hurt. Not "Charlie bit me" hurt. More like "Charlie stole my friggin' kidney" hurt.

I will admit to you, and you may not believe me, but the first thought that ran through my mind was not my wife or children, not my own safety, but this: How will I get tomorrow's newsletter out if I'm incapacitated? Can I crawl to my laptop? Are my hands okay? Yes they are, all is well. As it turns out, my ample barrel chest and hip broke the fall before my hands came into play.

Can I stand up? I'm ashamed to tell you that I was truly afraid to try. What if it hurt? It's kind of like when you wash your privates with soap, and then when you go to pee, it burns. So you hold your pee because you know it will hurt. Just like that. I can take pain, I just can't take the anticipation of pain. If I were captured by our enemies, I fear I'd sing like a yellow-bellied canary at the mere sight of a sharpened golf tee.

I also have the thought — maybe seen on Bear Grylls' stupid show where he pretends to live in the wilderness killing crocs with a blowgun that he claims to have carved from a bamboo stick, but actually sleeps in a Ritz-Carlton while lackeys buy the blowgun on Amazon.com — but anyway, Bear says that if you think your back is broken, don't get up because then you may sever your spinal column, which is crucial for getting around. But it was my hip and maybe a few ribs that hurt. Then again, I think Bear says don't get up if your ribs are broken too, because they can slice through your innards and blood vessels like razors and you bleed to death internally. Stupid show.

I stared at the underside of the toilet and thought of how much it looks like a pregnant woman's tummy, which is another piece of knowledge to file away, though not necessarily helpful in my predicament. My eyes rolled around the place, taking it all in like Bear would do. *I wonder what's on the history of my laptop's internet browser. I should probably format my hard drive if I ever make it that far. Are there bank accounts anywhere that I should let Lulu know about? Sadly, no. Hey, the mini-bar is almost in reach, I wonder how much the pistachios are?* These are the thoughts that race through your brain when you're prostrate, naked as a walrus on the cold floor of your hotel room with unknown broken bones. In case you were wondering.

Finally I hauled myself up on all fours and crawled to my bed. I figured if I'm going to die from internal bleeding, I might as well go out of this world like I entered it, swathed in thousand-count Turkish cotton sheets.

I lay there staring at the ceiling for maybe thirty minutes. To call the wife or not? That was first thing to enter my mind … when in trouble with my ribs, call the rib. I weighed the pros and cons. There's nothing she can do, and if I called her, it will just worry her, or worse, she may insist on getting the hotel staff to come help me or something, and that was out of the question for reasons I've already discussed. I called her anyway, because I can't help myself. Thankfully, she didn't answer.

Should I call Megan, my top lieutenant at the company? No, this isn't work-related, and it would creep her out if she knew I was calling her in the buff, which necessarily would have to come to her knowledge. Maybe my friend Joe Staffel who lives in LA? No, I didn't tell him I was in town because I had a lot of work things to do — he might get his feelings hurt if he knew — of course I guess now he knows. Sorry Joe, I was there for a few days for work, and didn't call you in advance to get together, but certainly considered calling you when I needed a friend in an emergency. Yes, I'm a shitty friend. But I'm still a friend, no?

So I lay there and stared at the ceiling.

Think, Harry, think.

The one thing that stupid fat-face limey Bear Grylls does say is that you should visualize a goal — staying alive, or in my case, getting home without too much humiliation — into little baby steps, and take it one little baby step at a time. The first step, I decide, is to get some clothes on. If

I'm appropriately clothed in jeans and a nice pressed white oxford shirt, it takes away all my issues about Lulu getting help from the hotel staff, or calling Megan, and it may help my self-esteem in general (there was a giant mirror on the wall next to my bed that, no matter how hard I tried, I couldn't stop glancing at). So I made an attempt at standing up. I slid to the edge of the bed, put my feet on the floor, and attempted to raise my torso, which is like raising the Titanic in more ways than one.

Holy shitola, jesu christo chinga tu madre! Yes, it hurt by God, but surprisingly, not as much as I thought. The anticipation, as I said, is always much worse than the actual pain. And without the pain, there is no sweet, or so I've heard. I stood up.

Hey, this isn't so bad. I put my clothes on — ever, ever so delicately and slowly. Leaning over hurt, but once I got my pants on, gravy. I started to feel better. I went ahead and worked on my computer and get the next day's issue mostly done, just in case. Now what? I felt better, so I called Lulu and told her my story, with obvious omissions, to make me more of a hero, which is to say I lied about almost everything.

I had a beer reception scheduled that night ... to attend or not? I chose to respectfully decline, and instead listened to a blues trio in my hotel lobby.

As the band struck up "Mack the Knife," I contemplated, Bear Grylls-style, my next challenge. I had to fly across the country, with a layover, early the next morning.

My plan was to get lots of cash out of the ATM and just pay everybody to get my suitcase into the cab, into the airport, into ticketing, and on the damn plane. Luckily I was going to be in first class so I could lay there like a board, stretched out.

On arrival, I would just pay a bell cap to put my bag in my car (the first healthy male under forty to ever ask for that service in thirty years, and my suitcase is a small rollerbag). I would then fly like a daffodil on a hurricane to Dr. Tonga to get his expert prognosis. I had a sneaking suspicion that there was a cortisone shot in my near future. Dr. Tonga doesn't bother my insurance company or the government with expensive x-rays (he doesn't take insurance or Medicare anyway). Besides, there's nothing you can do about broken or bruised ribs, except an eighty-dollar cortisone shot of course.

The next day, I followed my formula for getting from hotel to airport to airplane to home with nary a hitch, save for the nagging pain and — maybe worse — a nagging thought: How could I let myself get shoehorned into being the head coach of the kids' basketball team? I'm clearly too old for that.

GETTING KICKED OUT OF COSTA RICA

HAVE YOU EVER SPENT any significant time in a jail in Costa Rica? Well, now you can check that off your bucket list, because I've done it and will tell you all about it. You know, to save you the trip.

When my wife's brother asked me to tag along on a fishing trip to Costa Rica with some friends, I jumped at the opportunity. What a nice long weekend it would be, fishing for the elusive marlin along the best waters in the world for saltwater billfish.

We arrived in Costa Rica on Wednesday evening and we got in line to go through customs. No problem. I've been through customs in dozens of countries all around the world. I've always prided myself on my innocent face and simpatico karma that makes me glide through international borders like a greased pig on a frozen pond.

Oh, but my cockiness caught up with me with a vengeance. I, brilliant contrarian that I am, got into a slightly longer line at customs that I believed would actually run faster based on the fact that the silver-haired customs agent checking passaportes (as they call them in Español) was dressed very smartly in a nice blazer and was probably more intelligent and speedy than his compadres. I pointed this out to my friends.

"I am a world traveler, you see," I said, dropping a wink. "I know how to work these lines, eh?"

This was mistake number one, in retrospect.

But let's back up a mite. Perhaps mistake number one was when I returned home from a business trip last year to attend a party for San Antonio Spurs center Steve Kerr, who was retiring from basketball. That party was very fun as I recall, as we all ended up in the pool in our clothes playing — what else? — water basketball with several Spurs players. If you're a friend, relative, or the guy who stood behind me in line at Starbucks, you may recall that I bragged endlessly about hitting an outside shot against the three-point superstar, making me a three-point superstar … in water basketball. If this were a TV movie, which it may one day be (you never know), there would now be a close-up of my passport in my back pocket, with pool water flowing over it.

But really, if we want to truthfully trace back to mistake number one (there are really so many mistakes, we might have to go all the way back to shortly after my birth when I hit my head on a Jeep bumper), it may be when I took Lulu and her friend Dacia (yes, it's a stripper name, and no, she's not a stripper) to sushi lunch and announced that I was going to the paradise of Iraq for a few days with Diageo, the world's largest producer of spirits, to help administer humanitarian relief to hospitals in the wake of the war, back when it was deemed safe, about forty-eight hours after we had taken Baghdad.

While I do not regret that trip, as we did provide 90,000 pounds of medical supplies to ailing Iraqi hospitals (and some beer for the troops), it had the unfortunate consequence of providing many suspicious-looking visas being stamped into my passaporte. You know, friendly tropical vacation hotspots like Costa Rica don't welcome cool-faced civilians in wind jackets who frequent Beirut, The Hashemite Kingdom of Jordan, and particularly the recently liberated Republic of Iraq.

So getting back to my mistakes: I end up in the pool with the Spurs where my passaporte gets wet and soggy. That's mistake number one. Going to Iraq with Diageo was mistake number two, if you don't count the head wound on the jeep bumper.

Then not going to the post office to get a new passaporte because mine looks as if it's been through the spin cycle in the washer before being put in the microwave before being run over by a tractor before being chewed on a Cherokee squaw ... that was mistake number three.

So there I was, all smart and sassy, picking the silver-haired sharp-dressed man who would clearly recognize an honest American tourist with lots of U.S. dollars in his pocket to spend on the fledgling local economy.

This was mistake number four, because it turned out that this prick would make Alan Greenspan look like a drug-addled party boy. He gives my passaporte the equivalent of an anal search. He peels back laminate, splits pages looking for microscopic pieces of ... what? Nano-guns? Puts it under some kind of special light, probably just regular fluorescent trying to scare me. He frowns and shakes his head and clucks his tongue. Meanwhile my entire crew has made it through customs like a breeze and is on their way to get the rental car.

Then it happened. He was already suspicious of me and was searching for the straw that would break my marlin fishing weekend's back when he spotted the Arabic stamps in the back: Iraq, Jordan, Beirut, Amsterdam (they have hashish there I'm told) and various other disreputable countries like Australia, which is full of drunks.

"Mmm, no bueno," he said.

Now I'm not linguist, but at that point I knew I was in trouble. And when you are in trouble with a customs official — particularly in Central America where democracy is kind of a new experiment that they aren't completely settled on yet — and even if you are totally innocent, I'm here to tell you that bullets of sweat break out on your forehead, which make you appear all the more guilty.

"Mmm," he said again. But this time, a curious crowd is watching and another senior manager has arrived. This immigration official speaks friendly English, as they do in the Spanish markets in west

San Antonio when they wish to sell trinkets, and said that they will have to take the passaporte to another place to inspect it, and will I please sit down and wait, no problem. Now this sounded friendly, so I sat and waited.

One hour passes. Tick tock. Two hours pass. I remember reading a tourism poster in the terminal that said, "Time goes slow in Costa Rica!" Wow, they weren't kidding. Meanwhile, my brother-in-law and friends had no idea what's happened to me and nobody would let them back through, nor would they let me send them a message that I was going to be detained, maybe for fear that I'd hide a file in the note or something?

Later some of my so-called friends indelicately insinuated that for this to have happened I must have been rowdy drunk, wearing a sombrero, loudly singing Irish folk songs and insulting everybody within earshot. That was simply not the case. I slept the entire plane ride down there and was mild as a field of clovers.

Finally another immigration official arrived, with no English to make it more of a challenge — nay — opportunity for me. He declared sharply that I was to leave the country the next day, and that I was to wait in a spare white room all night with an armed guard until such time that I would be summoned.

Huh?

No Miranda warning? No court-appointed attorney? But most seriously, no iPod or book? I had so many questions I didn't even know where to start, or how to start, as my Spanish is a little rusty. Maybe he told me that the grateful government of Costa Rica is going to pay for my stay at the Los Suenos Resort until transportation back to the States can be arranged?

My interpretation turned out to be a bit optimistic. A guard escorted me to a plain white room with a single plastic chair, in which I sat before he did.

~*~

"Ah, senor, mi amigo, donde esta mi passaporte y equipage?" I asked, trying to make friends at first as I see him as the only obstacle between me and a pay phone. The guard shrugged and said what he will repeat several times throughout the night: "No se, senor." I don't know.

Can I use a phone? No se. Can I get my passport back? No se. Can I speak to a supervisor who speaks English? No se. Can I contact the U.S. consulate? No se. Can I get a drink of water? No se. Can I take this chair and shove it up your ass? No se.

By that time, my friends had bribed a janitor to sneak his cell phone to me (guard didn't seem to care) and I was able to tell them that I was detained and that they could go on without me, because I wisely suspected at this point that the golden shores of Costa Rica were beyond my capabilities.

Yet another immigration official (the bureaucracy in this freaking country is amazingly large for a so-called "republic" that is most famous for abolishing its military) came and he was all smiles and handshakes. He was the good cop. He kept repeating, "No worries, theeese is jest a reality. Eees okay, no problem, jees a reality. Wee send you home mañana, no problem, a reality, no worries, we happy, no?"

Well, no, not really actually. I couldn't really say with candor that I was "happy," per se. Fishing for billfish on the open seas makes me happy. Seeing my children again would make me happy. Drinking warm water from a dirty tap would have made me happy at that point. But sitting in a white room in a plastic chair with an armed guard all night doesn't usually make me particularly freaking happy.

"Oh, si," all smiles and nodding, so that I was tempted to kick his nuts up through his mouth. "Eeees jus a reality, my friend. No problem, a reality."

I think he meant to say "formality," but in a way his word was more descriptive of the situation, because that white room and that plastic chair and that armed guard were my true reality. We were at about midnight at that point, and I experienced what my consultants refer to as a "paradigm shift" after contemplating my situation from a higher sphere. My thinking, attitude and demeanor shifted from indignant pissed-off haughty journalist U.S. citizen with inalienable rights to foreign captive jackass without a gun or passport who'd better start playing nice. So I didn't kick him, because at this point it occured to me that I might have been walking the fine line between just leaving the country quietly or going to a more permanent dank prison ruled by a sodomite named Guapo. I chose a conciliatory tone and offered him and the guard fancy American Orbit gum from my pocket, the new tangy orange flavor they wouldn't get in Costa Rica for two more years.

Finally, at 6:00 a.m., and maybe just because of the gum, I was allowed a phone call on a pay phone that looks as if Castro had forged it from old rusty cannon balls just after taking over Cuba, and painted it a nice Soviet shade of drab green. I called Lulu (collect) and instructed her to contact Continental Airlines and get me the first flight out, preferably first class, and to tell the airline to send a beefy agent to fetch me from the holding room so we could make a break for the gate. She did this, and Continental told her that the government of Costa Rica has already informed them that they want me out of their country ASAP (they'd already arranged my ticket), so there would be no problem in me getting to the gate. She upgraded me to first class, bless her tall blond soul.

At 7:30 a.m., two armed guards escorted me to the plane, all the way to my seat in 2A. As they turned to go, I gave them my best Jim Carrey impression: "Thanks for the memories, can't wait to return! Oh, and don't forget to write." Or something to that effect. The other passengers were either impressed or horrified. I actually said something saltier than that, but I'll spare you the details, as it wasn't my finest hour to folks who were just doing their job.

~*~

The government of Costa Rica, such as it is, had requested that I never return to their fair country. Finally, we agreed on something! Happy days. You know, I felt this was a healthy start towards a reconciliation. It's like saying we both like *Breakfast at Tiffany's*. It's a small but solid cornerstone on which to forge our future together, me and Costa Rica.

They tore up my passaporte to such a degree that I actually had a little trouble getting back into the blessed beautiful United States. Birth certificates and Social Security cards had to be faxed from courthouses, bags had to be searched (again), and more indignities endured. But I got back to the blessed U.S., where they have habeas corpus, a right I hadn't fully appreciated until then.

So why am I public enemy number one in Costa Rica? I'm not entirely certain, but I think those Inspector Clouseaus know a small arms dealer when they see one.

"You're a beer writer," one official had asked in disdain. "A beer writer? Mmm." He'd seen too many *Murder, She Wrote* and *Matlock* episodes to believe that a beer writer would travel to Jordan, where beer is practically illegal.

The official reason was because they felt beyond a reasonable doubt that my passaporte had been tampered with, and in fact I was not who I said I was. Why anybody would pretend to be me, Harry Schuhmacher, a beer journalist from San Antonio, is beyond me. But apparently everybody wants to be me when trying to get into Central American countries.

I've since learned that Costa Rica is a destination of choice for felons on the run, and tampered passports are the best way to get into the country.

The frayed passaporte, the Arabic, my boots with Arabian sand on them, an iPod with U2, a sarcastic wit and a foul mouth … it proved a combination that was just too much: I showed all the traits of a desperado on the lam, not fit for the unarmed waifs of Costa Rica.

So the marlin remained safe from my hooks, but my bed was not. I went to sleep for twelve hours straight.

DOLPHIN ROCK

WHEN I WAS A kid I had a friend whose grandfather had a ranch near town. This ranch had an unusual "feature": a huge limestone outcropping, about a hundred feet high (or so it seemed to a child) that looked like a giant gray phallus-shaped dolphin coming out of a grassy ocean at a forty-five-degree angle to play ball with the sun. Here's my expert rendering of it:

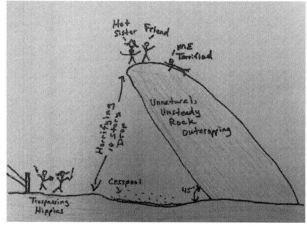

As you can plainly see, it is a horrifying monolith. For one, it stuck at such an angle that I was always afraid it would tip over; two, it had a disgusting cesspool at its base that bred skeeters and snakes; and three, my friend and his hot older sister who always wore a bathing suit constantly insisted on climbing it and peering over its edge. They called it, innocuously enough, Dolphin Rock (although I may have dreamt that later). I always imagined a more sinister name, like Devil's Nose or Mocking Gravity.

Not only that, but this unnatural, unsteady, terrifying outcropping stood at the corner of my friend's property, so that hippies from a nearby dope smoking camp (or something) would regularly trespass to scale the rock and drop their beer cans over the edge and soak in the sun like lizards.

As each school week progressed I would pray that my friend would not suggest that we go to his grandfather's ranch, because I knew we'd be scaling that godforsaken barren rock, and again I'd be humiliated in front of his hot-older-sister-in-a-bathing-suit and her hot friends who would, like my friend, just walk up the rock and dance at the top while I would crawl on my stomach like I was taking the next trench in World War I.

Heights were never my thing. I happen to subscribe to that old ditty that it's not the height that is the issue, and it's not even the falling — it's the impact. The bottom of my feet never touched Dolphin Rock, but I've shredded the front of many shirts on it.

On returning home my mother would usually say something comforting to ease my obvious suffering.

"What the hell! Do they drag you behind the jeep on your stomach when you're out there?"

"No," I'd say lamely as if that was a possibility.

I could never tell her that I had climbed — nay — belly-crawled a limestone rock that was ten-stories high against my will, because I knew she'd say something infuriatingly logical like, "If you don't like it, don't do it." But I was much too insecure not to join them, having a deep need to fit in and not appear weak, particularly in front of pretty-girls-in-bathing-suits, an insecurity I harbor to this day. Fortunately for my safety and sanity, I'm not friends with many cliff diving swimsuit models. Fortunately.

I would justify my cowardice by telling myself that I was smarter than my friend and his hot-older-sister-in-a-bathing-suit, because they obviously didn't grasp simple geometry, the theory of gravity and its inverse square, and how cantilevers work. Because if they had, they would understand that our weight would no doubt uproot the rock from its base eventually; and without this purchase, we'd necessarily go hurling into the cesspool below to a painful and — worse — messy death (all the while accelerating at a mortal rate of 9.8 meters per second squared, if in a vacuum. Yes, I was that kind of dork). And the cesspool presented a whole other set of horrors for me. As a child and now, I can't stand to be dirty. I dreaded going to birthday parties because I didn't like seeing the other children with cake icing around their mouths and their hands sticky with Hawaiian punch. As a baby I once cried for hours because I got honey on my neck. Fodder for the shrink in my future as soon as I can afford one.

What was most humiliating was how my friend and his hot-older-sister-in-a-bathing-suit would dance around on the peak of Death Rock and stand on the edge peering over at the cesspool below as I clung shaking in fear to the limestone. I still have nightmares about it to this day. At my own ranch we have a cliff that I have never gone anywhere near, yet I still weekly dream about driving my truck off it. Have I mentioned that heights aren't my thing? I get dizzy walking on the second level of malls, and don't get me started on the DFW Terminal D escalators.

It would be one thing if there was a deep blue lagoon at the bottom to jump into — that might be worth the danger and the effort. But to climb that terrifying rock just to look at a mud puddle — I just didn't see the risk-reward payoff. Even the drug-addled hippies grew bored with Dolphin Rock and stopped trespassing, which was a relief because my friend's grandfather insisted on calling the federal game wardens every time he spotted one, grumbling about "damn teenagers" and "no respect for property." It was quite a production and needless drama.

~*~

At one point, as my friend and his hot-older-sister-in-a-bathing-suit were dancing around and I was clutching the rock for dear life, I remember seeing my tears falling to the chalky limestone, drying almost instantly in the sun. Here I decided that enough is enough. But I didn't refuse to scale Dolphin Rock the next time they suggested it — oh no, that would be the healthy way to deal with the problem. I was raised differently. I simply started avoiding my friend in class, didn't return his calls, and ducked behind water fountains and dived under bleachers when I saw him. In other words, I simply ended the friendship due to that dreadful rock. I realize this makes me seem neurotic, poorly adjusted, passive-aggressive, and a little crazy. But there it is. There's no point in hiding it now.

An Occupational Hazard

IN A CONTINUOUS EFFORT to bring breaking beer news to all my gentle, loyal readers, it's necessary to do two things: travel and drink, both of which can wind up having negative consequences.

At the time, business was booming for your humble beer journalist, and as such, I was traveling extensively: I went to Denver, Des Moines, New York, and Germany in a single month. Winter was cruelly upon us and there was never a spare minute or a warm clime for this hot-blooded Texan. And Europe is the worst. One thing about Western Europe is that we Yanks tend to equate it with the U.S. in terms of climate, we all being representative democracies and all. What we forget is that Europe is generally on the same latitudinal parallel as Nova Scotia, so yeah, it's kind of cold.

This is something I know very, very well … now.

When I toured Bavaria that year with a troupe of beer trade journalists, all I managed to bring were old leather-soled bathroom slippers, flimsy khaki slacks from Target, and a discarded barn coat from the ranch fashioned from burlap. I thought since Bavaria was in southern Germany it would be mild. A simple Google weather check would have gone miles toward disavowing me of this delusion and would have prevented a tremendous amount of discomfort and injury. To say I was not outfitted appropriately was a gross understatement as we slogged from one cold dank brewery to another in the snow. I blamed my rib Lulu of course, who sent her absentminded charge packing to Germany in November for a week without so much as glancing inside my bag to see what I packed, or more importantly what I failed to pack.

"In my view that is gross negligence as a wife and demonstrating an obvious disregard for my well-being, and possible intentional harm, but I'll leave that up to my lawyer," I told her on a transatlantic phone call from my hotel room.

"Uh-hummm."

I got the impression she was chewing gum and doing her nails.

In case you don't know, breweries are necessarily vertical in their construction, particularly old Bavarian breweries, because they utilize the reliable force of gravity to transfer the golden nectar from brew kettle to lauder tun to fermenter to, finally, barrels in an underground cave (I may have the sequence wrong, but I'm pretty sure the barrels in the cave are last). So touring a brewery necessitates navigating flights upon flights of beer-soaked stairs carved in stone. With my leather slippers barely gaining purchase on even a rough surface, I was constantly falling down. Already uncoordinated in the best of circumstances, there was not a wet stair, a patch of black ice, a snow bank, or a dank fermenter floor in Bavaria that failed to trip me up. At one brewery I slid down about fifty stairs on my bottom, ripping the backside of my barn coat. The brewery owner was wailing bloody murder in German, not for my safety mind you, but because I suspect he smelled a lawsuit coming from such a scantily clad vagabond who obviously doesn't have two nickels to rub together. About halfway through the tour, our German guide was convinced that I was mentally disabled, and took to assisting me in and out of the bus like an invalid child and addressing me in a loud, slow tone normally reserved for simpletons. I overheard him whisper to a hop grower as he glared down on me after I fell for the fifth time that morning, "Er ist retardiert." My German's a little rusty, but I got the drift of his meaning. The farmer nodded with sympathy as he helped me up. The other journos thought it hilarious, and the epithet stuck for the rest of the trip.

The other main difficulty I had in Germany was the gas. At one point at a formal dinner with the Faust family, prominent brewers in Bamberg, after I shrilly broke wind for the third time and couldn't in good conscience continue to pretend nobody heard (it shook the window panes), I felt obliged to offer an apology and explanation.

"Wow," I said, red-faced, "must be this altitude. In Texas we're not used to being up this high."

I know, kind of lame.

"Sir, we're at sea level," our German guide quietly informed me.

Again, where is Google when you need it?

I briefly considered playing up my newfound reputation of mental incapacitation, but I did have some semblance of pride. Anyway, the Faust brothers are gentlemen and accepted my excuse at face value; perhaps our guide pre-briefed them of my "retardiert"? Anyway, you may think your merry correspondent is exaggerating. I assure you, if I am, not by much. Just ask any of my colleagues on the trip and they will corroborate. It's embarrassing, I know, but this confession is therapeutic.

The problem, of course, is all that purple cabbage and schnitzel and beer they're forever stuffing in your gob for breakfast, lunch, afternoon cake, and supper. Yes, Germans drink beer at breakfast like we drink coffee. And you can't politely refuse a German lest they take offense if you don't relish and gorge on every entrée and beer like some half-starved Philistine after a forced march. Who the hell else but a German would think that purple cabbage is an edible dish? It's like eating greasy lemon grass, and blows you out just as grass does a heifer. At one restaurant, they served a fried glob of fat inside an onion covered in gravy, an egg, butter, and bacon, accompanied by, what else? A big steaming mound of purple cabbage, along with endless pints of some kind of vile lager of their own invention that they smoked like pork. My bowels screamed for days. The bus rides were a cacophony of German flutes, and I'm ashamed to admit I was by far the worst offender even with my Teutonic constitution.

At one point we were to dine with some sort of German royalty, a bloated viscount or duke or something, in his drafty heatless stone castle on a desolate windswept hill, and our guide saw fit to pull me aside to politely implore me to try to gain control of myself "for his majesty's sake." It was day five of being plied with nothing but wiener schnitzel, the ever-present purple cabbage, and about a half barrel of beer per person per day, so I did the best I could under these trying circumstances. Unfortunately, you can't clap a stopper on Mother Nature, as the saying goes. But I doubt I scandalized the good duke, for I'm convinced even royalty aren't immune to flatulent episodes every now and then. And besides, he was stone deaf.

~*~

By day seven I was again myself (you eventually either die of dysentery or you buck up get used to it), and my colleague Pete Reid, the publisher of *Modern Brewery Age*, lent me some wool socks and my guardian angel Julie Bradford at *All About*

Beer lent me her daughter's gloves, which if I recall were purple with pink stitching. I endeavored to persevere as we trudged from one identical brewery to another over snow banks and through long patches of black ice, pretending to marvel at yet another identical fermentation tank. A few more falls and a few more farts, and the trip was over. It was a great time, and by the time my plane touched down in London for a business meeting, I felt oddly refreshed and spry, like a spent balloon, and that's a good thing because I was about to have a pleasant run-in.

But first, a word of advice: This may surprise you, but when I was a child I was painfully shy. I was terrified of meeting new people, and would be happy as a clam if just allowed to lock myself in my room 24/7 and watch *M*A*S*H* reruns for the rest of my life.

Shyness is a terrible trait for a guy to have. It keeps you from excelling at work, it keeps you from making new friends, and worst of all, it keeps you from getting laid. So about halfway through college I decided to teach myself not to be shy, and the only way to do that effectively was to drink more beer. If I hadn't discovered beer, I wouldn't have had the courage to speak to Lulu, and today I'd be a sad lonely old man of forty-five.

When I started my company and became a journalist, I had to take it to the next level, and not only not be shy but be an extrovert — give speeches in front of hundreds of beer distributors, make new contacts and sources, eat with my hands in front of people. Again, beer came in mighty handy.

Today I am decidedly not shy, and it's liberating. I still get nervous around new people sometimes, and I am forced to push through it and remember to smile and engage and be clever. It has served me well.

So if you're shy like I was, my advice is to just man up and get over it. They can't eat you. My mother also told me that. And my old friend August Busch IV once told me, "Making friends is our business." Indeed.

For instance, after meetings in London, I was sitting with my friends Kaumil and Chewy at an outdoor patio bar for a dinner that was blessedly absent of cabbage of any kind. Kaumil was a beverage and tobacco analyst with UBS, and Chewy owns a chain of pharmacies in London. They got to talking about stocks and bonds and sports or whatever men talk about, and of course my mind wandered. I noticed that the table next to us was getting rowdy. I leaned over to them and said, "Hey, either you guys pipe down, or let us join you." They invited us over.

One among them was a pretty Brit with huge blue eyes and a bubbly personality. She said she was a TV host on the BBC and, judging from the stares of everybody in the bar, it occurred to me that she must be some sort of celebrity. I told her I was from Texas and she frowned.

"I'm sorry. I've been to Lubbock for a film shoot and it was horrible. It made me start smoking." I told her that this was a perfectly normal response to being in Lubbock … you must find an outlet, any outlet, when in that dusty dry town. I said I used to smoke when in Lubbock but stopped because, after all, it's bad for you — both smoking and Lubbock. She asked me how I was able to stop smoking. I looked her in the eye and said in earnest: "Cocaine." Her laugh was like the tinkle of tiny bells.

Many other little jokes like that were told to illicit more tiny bells. Pretty soon she was seated by my side and cooing over me and playing with my hair. The fastest way to a pretty girl's heart is either through food or humor, and since I didn't have any food at hand, well …

Her date — a guitarist in a band who was much younger than she or I — watched with benign interest from across the table. He spoke in a northern England York accent that might as well have been Greek, for it was completely unintelligible to me. In response to the few words he said (he was shy, you see), I just smiled and repeated, "Righty-o mate." What else was I to do? All in all it was great fun save for an gnawing ache in my wrist, likely the result of constantly falling down in the snow while in Bavaria, I thought.

At the end of the meal, she asked that we retire to her flat for cocktails, but we ultimately paid our tab and left for our hotel, as my mother once told me that nothing good happens after midnight.

Later I discovered that she is not only famous, but infamous from when a girly magazine had her naked image projected gloriously onto the side of Parliament a few years ago, scandalizing the older MPs as they trudged to Whitehall in the early morning hours. So within five hours of arriving in London I was whooping it up with a celebu-bunny, one of Maxim magazine's 100 Hottest Women, and a true delight to behold. Yes, I'm a sucker for pretty women. That's just one benefit of losing my childhood shyness.

~*~

When I finally made it back to San Antonio, my wrist was aching in a way that I could no longer ignore, which put me in a sour mood, because this meant that I would have to do something I hate — and do you know what I hate? While you didn't ask, I'll tell you anyway. I hate doctors, except mine. I'll get to that in a minute, because I just thought of something else I hate even more than doctors. I hate pharmaceutical ads. All pharmaceutical ads. But what I REALLY despise, so much that I sometimes gag, are pharma ads for men. Drug ads targeting middle-aged men to treat things like going potty too much, gummy arteries, and flabby weeners may be effective in selling the drugs, but the ads invariably feature dough-faced imbeciles doing stupid things.

I hadn't been back in the glorious U-S-of-A for too long before I saw an ad featuring a smug asshole whining that he has to pee three times a night. Oh, boo-hoo. People are eating babies in Sub-Saharan Africa, but let's drop everything and spend precious Medicare dollars so you don't have to haul your ass to the toilet so much. Ever heard of a chamber pot, or an empty two-liter Coke bottle? Use some ingenuity, man.

But now, with LookMaNoPee™, he lives a great life with reduced bathroom breaks — cue the shots of him riding a bike with his ugly wife. He's the one wearing a helmet. Safety first. So he takes a pill so he can hold his peepee until the morning, and he wears a helmet to protect his precious head in case he makes a boo boo while riding a bike — a bicycle, not a motorcycle, mind you. What a stud. John Wayne is sitting on a mantle of clouds somewhere throwing up into his Stetson in disgust, relieved that he's dead and doesn't have to live amongst such chicken livers. This guy won't need Viagra because I doubt it would ever occur to his wife, even as ugly as she is, to bed such a nancy-boy. Drug ads always have these shots of smiling middle-aged people in hideous sweatpants doing the most inane things: flying a kite, jogging in a marathon, riding bikes, and my favorite: setting balloons free. What are you, seven? And then they wave at them, like idiots — expecting the balloons to what? Wave back?

And have you seen the ad where the doctor is explaining to his patient the side effects of whatever drug they're selling, as required by law? The patient looks suitably fascinated in the knowledge that the drug could cause his eyes to bleed hydrochloric acid, his rectum to leak Hawaiian Punch, and in "extremely rare cases," his belly button to spontaneously shoot flaming arrows. The patient nods like a Mandarin doll — excited about the possibility of bleeding acid just so he won't wet the bed anymore — with a rapt look on his face, as if he's so appreciative that his doctor shares this crucial information with him. If my doctor even started to bore me with the side effects of the rainbow of drugs I currently take, I would walk out after hurling a urine-filled two-liter Coke bottle at him.

But Dr. Tonga would never do that. In the Abidjan, on the Côte d'Ivoire in Africa, where he received his education according to the "degree" on the wall, they apparently teach a better bedside manner than our medical institutions. And they eat babies in Abidjan, lacking other protein that's handy, so consequently Dr. T treats me and all his patients with the appropriate level of hostility earned by those of us who are privileged and coddled. When I complain of debilitating pain in my left hand, Dr. T. screams at me that it's my fault for typing so much. When I yell back at him that I am a writer, and so if he wants to keep getting paid, he'd better make sure I can keep typing, he finally writes a prescription — reluctantly — for an anti-inflammatory, and his nurse/secretary/housekeeper pulls down my pants and gives me a cortisone shot in my bottom, though I can tell he believes me to be a pansy.

I like Dr. Tonga. He doesn't take any crap, and he doesn't take insurance. Just pay your hundred bucks and he'll treat any ailments you have — in my case high blood pressure, carpal tunnel, chronically reoccurring pneumonia, broken feet, asthma, allergies, hypochondria, bloating, and gas — and my life insurance company is none the wiser. All of these ailments, including and especially hypochondria, Dr. Tonga treats with cortisone shots. He is of the belief, taught to him by the wise elders of the Haitian medical community, that cortisone is the cure-all for everything, from gas to gout. And you know what, damned if he's right. It doesn't take a Harvard medical school grad to goose up your patients with steroids. I'm convinced Dr. Tonga is the future of medicine in this country: inexpensive, effective, no-nonsense health care, without all the needless accoutrements, like clean needles and licensed nurses. And he doesn't keep me waiting since I've never seen another patient there. He respects my time. And you can smoke cigars in his waiting room. While Dr. T doesn't speak much English, we understand each other. I hate doctors, and he hates patients. It's a symbiotic relationship.

Okay, tirade over. Like I was saying, the wheels had finally come off the train by the time I got back from eating globs of fat stuffed in onions in Germany, but this was actually a long time coming. Since I'd turned forty, it all went downhill very fast. First it was a horrible bout of pneumonia which laid me under for a full month, a persistent rash, accelerated hair loss, and then a painful ache in my left hand which had been like having red hot razors in my wrist joint which only hurt when I typed and took a breath, for going on twelve weeks. Oh, and I couldn't thread a fishing line through a hook eye anymore without squinting my eyes.

Dr. Tonga had taken it all in stride, administering cortisone shots like a punch-drunk NFL team doctor, God bless his Haitian soul. But under pressure from my rib, I reluctantly agreed that my many ailments had finally, predictably, outpaced his abilities — his Caribbean remedies (rum and cigars to treat pneumonia, for example) simply can't keep up with my northern Atlantic afflictions. When the last steroid shot failed to diminish the swelling in my wrist even nominally, I knew that, sadly, my days of watching Ricky Lake reruns on the black and white TV in his waiting room were limited. And my hands are kind of important, given that I type two thousand words a day for my job, not including emails and blog posts.

So I had my rib call around to find a new general practitioner who preferably has a medical degree from this country. Lordy, we must have a serious shortage of GPs, because nobody would accept me as a new patient. And think of how much worse it will get under the government's universal health coverage when even hobos are allowed to see doctors.

I finally got in to see a GP but only because a mutual friend (thanks Lynnette) of the doc begged her to see me. Yes, my new doctor is a female, and I'm happy to report that she is an attractive female (not that that matters, of course). I anticipated my first date, er, appointment with Dr. Sandra Gonzalez with equal parts anxiety and exhilaration — anxiety because she might ask me to disrobe, and exhilaration because she might ask me to disrobe. So many questions: should I spray tan, trim up, get a tattoo?

Turns out it didn't matter because the first date/appointment was with her physician's assistant, who drew blood and X-rayed my wrist and tapped around on my chest listening to the remnants of my bronchitic lungs — but did not ask me to disrobe. The doctor was so busy that I had to make another appointment to get the benefit of her diagnosis and treatment. This is a far cry from Dr. Tonga, who would have palmed me twenty hydrocodone and a steroid shot and had me out the door in the time it took this physician's assistant to take my temperature ("Treat 'em and street 'em" is Tonga's motto). I want to be "streeted" by Tonga, not warehoused by Gonzalez.

Two days later my rib and I are sitting on the back patio of StoneWerks, a local watering hole, drinking beer in the sun. She has her feet up on the firepit like a boy. "So," she says, "how was Dr. Gonzalez?"

"You know what, Lulu? I feel like I don't have a lot of time to dicker around with doctors, especially pretty ones." I glance at her to gauge her jealousy. No change of expression, just the tiny turning down of the corners of her mouth — which likely was due to the slowness of our waiter. "And doctors like hotty Gonzalez have tight schedules and slowly practice careful, responsible medicine."

My rib looked at me over her sunglasses. "Harry," she said as I snuck a look at her legs (I, too, was wearing sunglasses), "Dr. Tonger…"

"Tonga!" I corrected.

"Whatever. He told you to smoke cigars when you had pneumonia. I mean, what kind of doctor would tell you that?"

I looked back at her face coldly. "Do not disrespect Dr. Tonga in my presence. Hate the game, not the doctor. He may not be my physician anymore, but by God, Dr. Tonga and I understand each other — which is the definition of love and respect."

Dr. Gonzalez ultimately said that I have the gout in my wrist, which is when you get razor sharp crystals in your joints from drinking too much beer, a necessary job hazard. The only cure at that point, since I had let it go so long (she said with a hint of disgust — Dr. Tonga had his faults, but he wasn't a judger), is to take large amounts of a drug called colchicine, which is a poison in the same line as arsenic. It's also called "Meadow Saffron" or "Satan's Revenge" in some circles. This toxic agent, when taken at the doses I had to, is so venomous that thirty minutes after ingesting the first pill it induces projectile vomiting and explosive diarrhea like a two-headed fire hydrant that would make a caveman blush. It also produces cold sweats, dizziness, rashes, clammy palms, blurry vision, confusion, a swelling and fever of the inner organs, achy teeth, et cetera, et cetera. But luckily for me, this wonder drug also cures gout somehow. The trick is to take enough of the vile stuff to cure the gout, but not enough to kill you. It's a fine line we colchicine takers walk.

I spent two days rolling around in a cold sweat on the bathroom floor clutching my gut and crying. But anybody who has had serious gout before will agree that I couldn't care less if it caused blood to flow from my eyes and my toes to fall off (something Dr. Gonzalez helpfully apprised me of during our visit), I would take it to get rid of the gout's horrible, horrible pain. Now if you'll excuse me, I'm going to put on my helmet and ride a bike and set off a bunch of balloons with my wife.

SHAKE N' BAKE

IN OCTOBER OF 2006, I was invited to speak on an Annapolis AM radio program about how to make it as an entrepreneur. What follows is how I imagined the interview going. And just to be clear, it did not, for better or for worse, go exactly this way, but I was actually nervous that someone would hear my honest answers to the prepared questions clearly geared toward classic self-improvement doctrines, straight out "The 7 Habits of.." And "Think and Grow Rich," and fall into despair.

Q: Good morning Annapolis! I'm Matt Malone and we're here in the studio with Harry Schuhmacher, the founder and publisher of *Beer Business Daily*. Harry, welcome to the program.

H: Thanks for having me.

Q: So, Harry, do you view "success" as a noun or a verb? A journey … or a destination?

H: Well, it's currently very much a verb, unfortunately, but I very much would wish it to be a noun. If Marvin Shanken suddenly appears on my doorstep with a check for $20 million to buy me out, I am so out of here and tanning my noun on a coral beach in the Keys.

Q: Heh, okay, that's um … good. So, did your family support your move to entrepreneurship?

H: Actually, no. We were constantly short of cash and my wife and children complained incessantly about it. Apparently they're too good for Campos Pinto Beans with Schuhmacher Secret Sauce five days a week. Today we are doing better (we now eat Bush's Baked Beans — with Schuhmacher Secret Sauce), but they still complain that I travel too much. Do you call that support, or attempted career sabotage?

Q: Uh —

H: I thought so.

Q: Right. Moving on. Can you tell our listeners how the epiphany occurred? When did the proverbial light bulb go off in your head to create your first beer publication?

H: I was sitting on the toilet reading the competition, and I thought, *Dang, he's good. I'll never be able to be as good as he is*. But I started it anyway, because I had no other options at the time, and struggled through five years of not beating him. Today, I still haven't beaten him. Consequently, I've now grown very accustomed to being a loser.

Q: Wow, very inspirational. But doesn't your competition drive you to higher spheres of excellence, Harry?

H: Not exactly. You see, I find that when my competitors experience victories over me, I break out the aluminum foil for my windows and curl up in the fetal position on my bed, shaking and weeping, sometimes for days on end. Sometimes I even suck my thumb, but that's for effect, not comfort — I never know when my wife might walk in. Or I fly to Las Vegas and blow thousands on gambling and whiskey.

Q: *(Chuckles nervously)*

H: Just kidding. I blow thousands on gambling and beer. Of course. You get the picture.

Q: Actually, I'm afraid I don't get the picture …

H: I've been pulling your leg, Mark. Yes, success IS a verb, and I'll never quit, EVER, because money is so transient and unimportant to me. You know how I keep it real, Mike? Here in my heart? *(Pounds chest gently with fist.)* Yessir, for this *hombre*, it's the challenge of climbing an impossibly high and freezing mountain that gets my juices a-flowin'. And when Debbie Downers say, "Hey, you can't climb that mountain, Harry, you're really out of shape and have asthma and short legs and no athletic ability," I reply, boldly, chin up, "Madam, I can and I WILL climb that mountain, simply because it's there, even if it kills me from an asthma attack and I leave my children fatherless and my wife penniless." And speaking of them, I just want to take this moment to thank my wife and three sons (Shake 'N Bake) for always being there when I needed them, and never asking for a dime when times were rough, and always eating beans and tortillas five days a week with nary a complaint. I love you, my gassy little bears. And now that I've reached the apex of my career, I want to especially thank my worthy competition for constantly driving me to perform at a higher level of excellence. Without you, I wouldn't have had the confidence to attempt to climb that mountain and die of hypothermia. God bless America, and a shout-out to my homeboy Alan Greenspan for keeping interest rates so low and for whoever invented the hi-def flat-screen LCD TV. Peace out, Annapolis.

REMEMBRANCE OF THINGS PAST

"WHEN NOTHING ELSE FROM the past subsists, after people are dead, after the destruction of things, smell and taste alone remain, like souls bearing resiliently, on tiny and almost impalpable drops of their essence, the vast edifice of memory."

These poignant words appear at the beginning of *In Search of Lost Time*, the eternal if not interminable biographical novel by Marcel Proust. Here the narrator remarks how scents possess such a strong power, unique amongst the senses, to transport you to a time in your past, often formerly forgotten episodes in childhood.

For Proust, that scent proved to be the sweet-tart smell of cake soaked in tea. For me, it's the smell of molded cardboard soaked in stale beer.

For going on four generations, my family, the Schuhmachers, had been carving their sustenance out of the arid lands of Texas as wholesale beer distributors. Some of my earliest memories are of playing hide-and-seek amongst stacks of beer in my father's warehouse in Houston. In a bustling commercial beer operation, tall pallets of beer are constantly in motion, so the child must be alert, lest he get run over by a forklift. But other than those trifling dangers, which necessarily heightened the excitement of the game, the beer stacks proved even better than a hedge maze for hours of entertainment for my sisters and me.

As in every beer warehouse, then and now, accidents happen. A forklift holding a pallet with sixty-five cases of longneck bottles of beer on it will hook a turn too fast, and the stack of beer necessarily falls to the ground based on the inverse square and Newton's theory of gravity, smashing about half the bottles. The result is a messy mountain of soaked cardboard, glass, and beer. This mountain is pushed by a forklift into a section of the warehouse called the "breaker pile."

This breaker pile varies in size and age at any given time, depending on how fast the workers in the breaker pile are able to "repack" the salvageable bottles and cans from those that are leaking or broken. The good cans and bottles are cleaned and repacked into cartons, while the rest is documented and destroyed (to regain the lost excise tax). It's a tedious and time-consuming job, as you're dealing with a lot of broken glass, stale beer, soggy cardboard, and those annoying tiny gnats that inevitably appear where there is spilt beer. But it's an important job: No beer must be wasted, not one single bottle.

The breaker pile is where the wise beer distributor owner first puts his children to work. He does this for several good reasons: First, the breaker pile is the worst job in the warehouse and as the children of distributors are perceived — usually correctly — as rich brats by the other employees, throwing them to the breaker pile forces the children to earn their salt early on. Second, children are good at working the breaker pile for some reason: Maybe it's their small hands, maybe it's the fact they are fearless amongst shards of glass, maybe it's their ability to make a game out of anything. But mostly I suspect it's because children are dumb and don't know any better.

So I spent my childhood summers washing the shards of glass off bottles, getting blisters on my thumb from "ringing" cans into those plastic six-pack rings, gluing new twelve-pack carriers, and stapling cases shut. The smell of a ripe breaker pile is a combination of seaweed on the beach, boiling coffee, and a wet puppy. It's not as disagreeable as you would think, but actually a very sweetly musty smell. Not too far, actually, from Proust's cake dipped into tea, if the cake was actually a day-old Ahi tuna.

Now I work as a beer journalist. My father sold his distributorship many years ago, orphaning me from the world of beer distribution forever. But my work takes me into many beer warehouses across the country, and each time I draw near to a breaker pile, it takes me back to my childhood. It's the most powerful link I have to a time of innocence and wonder.

CHRISTMAS CRIME

THEY SAY THAT DECEMBER is the most wonderful time of the year, and as far as I could tell around the end of last year, it was the most wonderful time of the year for at least two things. The first was burglary. The second was a beverage, and necessarily followed the first, but let's begin with burglary, because as it turns out, you have to start somewhere, and strangers taking your stuff seems as good a start as any.

The sight of seeing your car on blocks is a curious one first thing in the morning. Initially, your brain says, *Hmmm, what is this? A practical joke?* Pretty elaborate joke, you say? Listen, my friends bought a 600-pound Longhorn calf and had it delivered to my ranch on my 40th birthday, so yes, stranger things have happened. But then your brain discards the notion that it's a practical joke for the simple reason that it isn't funny, and my friends are funny.

My youngest son Wyatt, clad in his Barney pajamas, padded out the front door to where I was standing. He looked at Lulu's Suburban for a beat, then he looked up at me.

"Wha happen mama's car?"

"I — I don't know?" I replied. I still wasn't sure.

Finally, after several seconds, it became apparent that her car was missing its wheels because somebody had stolen them. And when I say wheels, I actually mean the entire wheel, including the tire. And when I say missing, I mean completely gone, with the car sitting on blocks right there in our driveway.

Yes, at some point during the night while we were sleeping, a group of thugs jacked up her car, took all four wheels off, and thoughtfully placed the car, ever so gently, on four bricks (we live in a nice neighborhood, so our thugs are gentlemanly).

It's a sick feeling, knowing that thieves, stranger thieves, were so close to your bedroom and taking something dear to you. I never knew how dear Lulu's wheels were until they were missing. But that sick feeling soon turned to anger. Having dirty thugs so close to your family does that to you. But I have to admit that anger was tempered by a touch of schadenfreude. I've never put too much time, effort, or money into the various cars I've owned. I used to own a Jeep Rubicon, split pea soup green with removable top and metal flooring, which was host to all kinds of dirt on the outside that helped to insulate a mouse that lived somewhere inside. It's not that I'm untidy. Before I passed it on to my middle son, the Jeep often doubled as a hunting vehicle at the ranch, with top off, so the inside was covered in our region's famed white caliche dust. So it didn't really look dirty or gritty, it mostly looked like I let loose with a few eight balls of coke, or more likely in my case, a big bottle of Gold Bond Medicated Powder™.

To me, cars are for getting around in, and a warm home for a rodent, and that's about it. Washing a car is such a colossal waste of time and money. It's like washing a dog — what's the point? It's just going to go do what dogs do best, which is go out and poop in the yard (without wiping), roll around in the mud, lick itself, and, not to put too fine a point on it, but it's just going to immediately get dirty again. Washing a car or a dog is such a futile exercise that it throws me into a depression just thinking about it.

My rib Lulu, who is from the manor born, always drives nice cars and always keeps her car irritatingly immaculate. Not a speck of Gold Bond inside or out. Every week she goes to this place called the Scrubby Tub, or something, which is the only place in town where criminals newly released from prison can find a job. The jailbirds clean the car, she gets it dirty, repeat.

Her immaculate car wouldn't be so irritating to me if she didn't constantly berate me on how "disgusting" my car is, inside and out. I do clean it occasionally. The one time I took it to the Scrubby Tub the mouse jumped out, and the so-called tough work-release criminals were too afraid to finish the job. But most of the time I let the car, like my dog, do what it does best: get dirty. As long as the radio works, I'm all good. (I don't change the oil very often either – that's for suckers who believe the propaganda of the oil companies who are, of course, in cahoots with Detroit. Cars only need oil every two or three years, those little red and orange lights on the dash be damned.)

Anyway, so it was with a little bit of sweet redemption to find that the wheels were missing off Lulu's car. But also, I had a few observations: The economy must have really been bad if there was enough of a market for used Suburban wheels. I mean, who steals the wheels off somebody's car? They weren't even the shiny expensive wheels with spinning rims and lights favored by ignoramuses who can't afford school supplies for their kids but somehow find the money to buy stolen wheels for their leveraged hot rods. Ours were just standard issue wheels, straight off the dealer's lot. The ignoramuses who got our wheels weren't even smart enough to get the showy kind.

I live in a sleepy little town, and this town's investigative cop, who we'll call Barney Fife, offered little to think we'll ever get the wheels back or catch the criminals. Captain Fife did tell us that this had happened dozens of times in our neighborhood over the last month. They only take wheels from 08/09 Suburbans and Tahoes and whatever the Cadillac version of those cars are called. Escaladas I think.

Ours was a simple Suburban. Apparently the wheels from these particular kinds of cars are highly prized by those who have nothing better to do than drive up and down Congress Avenue revving their engines on their low-riders.

So why did I feel redeemed that Lulu got the wheels stolen off her car? Captain Fife also revealed that they suspect the local car wash — yes, her beloved Scrubby Tub — is the nexus point of these crimes, because the criminals they employ can check your address on the insurance card while they're wiping that disgusting Armor All grease all over your dashboard so that after driving it you feel like you have been handling a stick of butter — and spraying noxious chemicals (aka "new car smell") on your seats, and plan their evil heist accordingly.

Here are the indisputable facts:

Fact: I have rarely had my car washed, which is why my car is dirty, but …

Fact: The Scrubby Tub criminals have therefore never had occasion to gawk at my address since the one time I was there a mouse thoughtfully attacked them, so therefore …

Fact: My car does have the benefit of having wheels, which help it get around town while …

Fact: Lulu went to the Scrubby Tub a few days ago …

Conclusion: Lulu's car remained stationary all day on blocks until the special tow truck came to take it to the dealer, who was elated because he finally made his first sale in two months, while I buzzed around town shopping and lunching with friends and flying a kite while she remained trapped at home watching the 111th Congress get sworn in on C-Span.

Sadly, Captain Fife and his merry band of Keystone Cops couldn't be bothered to question the malcontents who work at the Scrubby Tub because they were too busy giving us taxpaying residents tickets for rolling stop signs. Such is life.

I went down to do a little thuggery of my own, *CSI: San Antonio*-style. Call me Horatio. I wore sunglasses, blared "We Won't Be Fooled Again," and questioned the manager for a few minutes. He was sublimely unhelpful and my sunglasses failed to intimidate. He did look my Jeep over with a raised eyebrow and offered to wash it for free. I declined on principle.

But you can't really blame the criminals at the Scrubby Tub for carrying out these elaborate crimes. They are criminals, and criminals do what they do best: crime. Just like a car is always destined to get dirty, and why a dog is destined to lick himself, and why ignorant people will always put money into shiny rims for their leveraged cars while their children steal paper and pencils from their classmates, in a never-ending feedback loop. It's the natural order of things.

~*~

At the Beer Business Daily headquarters the next day, things got a little better. Kim brought in a nice Christmas gift from one of the brewers, a large porcelain beer stein with a pewter top that flips open with your thumb. Most people display these steins on their bookshelves, but I actually like to use them as drinking mugs. I immediately poured a beer in it and sipped as we had our weekly staff meeting, obnoxiously flipping the pewter top open and closed with each sip (so that no beer is wasted due to evaporation, I suppose; those Germans are so parsimonious), and giving a loud "Ahhhh" with every sip. "The beer tastes soooo good out of these steins. Mmmm."

The staff was annoyed—perhaps because it was ten in the morning, and the meeting was dragging on, what with the long draughts of brew I took between sentences from my new stein. But for pure theatrics, there's not much more fun to be had at ten than sipping beer at your desk from a brand-new (free) German beer stein as your thirsty staff looks on longingly ... just before the eve of Christmas holiday.

"Dang this beer is smooth out of a stein, and it stays so cold. You oughta try this ... oh, wait, there's no drinking on the job unless you're the publisher." Boy, I think I'm funny. At least somebody does.

I considered taking it to bars and restaurants. "Uh, waiter, will you please fill this five-pound stein with another five pounds of beer?" I'd say, winking to somebody at a nearby table. "I'm a professional, don't try this at home." I would be like those serious bowlers who bring their own ball. I'd carry my stein around in a specially formed leather bag with my initials on it. I'd show up at industry conferences demanding that my beer be poured into my German beer stein. It would count as one of my carry-ons at the airport. It could be classified as a weapon, as its sheer heft makes it the perfect bludgeon.

But that's just a crazy dream of mine.

The next day, that dream was almost dashed when I arrived to work to find that our offices had been — can you guess? — burglarized. Ah, holiday recession crime. The stuff nightmares are made of, no?

~*~

We walked into the office that morning to see that the back door had been kicked in and was swaying idly on its hinges.

Oh, no, I thought. *They must have taken everything.*

When you see a swaying door on its hinges, you know what you value most by what immediately pops into your mind. Naturally I thought of the stuffed parakeet — the one we named "Parakeet" — that Dos Equis gifted me for Christmas the previous year. Also the wooden ammunition box that Anheuser-Busch sent before they were sold to Belgians, the lacquered signed portrait of the Miller Lite catfight girls wrestling in a fountain in the middle of a European square (I know, that's class), and of course my Pilsner Urquell humidor — all my favorite pieces of swag sent in by breweries in the hope of getting a decent shake. And the office tricorn hat.

Yes, I bought I tricorn hat. It was an impulse buy, obviously — nobody buys a tricorn hat after any amount of serious reflection — but I found a great use for it as a motivational tool at the office. As a joke, whenever a staffer did something good — landing a new subscriber or breaking a big story — they got to wear the raggedy old tricorn hat for the day.

Oh, what big laughs we had, or rather, I had. It was similar to the beer-drinking stein that I lorded over them. Had the office tricorn hat been taken?

And most importantly, there's the beer. Our office is stacked with cases of craft beers that folks send from around the world as tasters. I raced into the office, screaming, "The beer, the beer!"

I was soon relieved to find that all of the beer was there. Parakeet remained in his cage, his cold steely dead eyes always creepily watching, the ammunition box still holding up the lacquered portrait of the catfight girls still wrestling in their eternal fountain of youth. All was undisturbed.

Megan, being the sensible one, noted that all of the computers, laptops, flat-screen monitors and printers were still present and accounted for, too.

"Oh, yeah," I muttered, petting Parakeet with a finger through its cage, "of course, the computers. That's a relief." Nothing was gone.

But when I sat at my desk (which is just a piece of glass held up by three kegs), I noticed a few strange things:

1. My rubbish pail was gone.
2. Two discarded old computer monitors that we kept in a closet were now under my desk at my feet.

3. The little 15-inch TV that sat on my credenza was gone.
4. My tricorn hat, which had previously been hanging on a hat rack, was sitting on the center of my desk.

Like any Inspector Clouseau, I began to piece the crime scene together based on my limited set of clues. It all came together: A drunk vagabond must have peeked into my window and seen my TV and monitors and thought, Hey, I bet I can get a few forties of Steel Reserve High Gravity for any one of those. So he gathered his strength and broke down our back door, which wasn't much of a door. Since he didn't possess a vehicle, he decided that he would take only what fit into my rubbish pail, because a hobo walking down the street carrying three flat-panel monitors might attract suspicion. So he found two unattached monitors in the closet and sat at my desk trying to put one, then the other, into the pail, but found that they were both too wide. Then he saw my little TV, and found that it indeed fit perfectly into the rubbish pail.

Then he did a walkabout, apparently. He opened several cases of craft beer, but decided that either the ABVs were too low or that warm Imperial Stout might not be very refreshing on a thirty-degree night. He then sat at my desk again, and my magnificent tricorn hat must have caught his intoxicated eye. He may have tried it on and admired his reflection in the glass of the monitor on my desk, but ultimately decided it didn't enhance his facial features. So he left it and slid back out the door onto the street with my little TV in my rubbish pail, a skip in his step as he thought of popping open that first cold Steel Reserve.

We got off easy. The TV was the cheapest piece of electronics in the office. Had he stole one laptop, he would have more than doubled his take of Steel Reserve. Incidentally, if he had bothered to look in the fridge, he would have found several Steel Reserves, ice cold and ready to go, saving him the inefficient exchange rate of bartering an aging 15-inch TV. I mean, he really must be a terrible vagabond, if there is such a thing as a good vagabond. He hit the jackpot when he broke into my office. It was full of high ABV beer, even cheap lager high-gravity beer chilled in the fridge, plus there were three twenty-dollar bills on my desk, untouched. No, it was the tricorn hat that drew his gaze, and he even left that jewel. Why he only relieved me of that crappy TV, I'll never know.

Incidentally, nobody wanted to wear the tricorn hat anymore, as I work in an office full of people who are obviously bigoted toward drunken thieving hobos. I actually think the tricorn had more value: It had crowned a homeless person's head. But my staff's irrational fear of lice trumps any show of humility or equanimity.

But any remaining chance the vagabond had of reclaiming the tricorn (or any other goods) was squashed the very next day. An alarm system was installed and my carpenter reinforced all the doors with metal brackets. Plus you couldn't step outside without seeing three or four SAPD cruisers. Here's why:

The policeman who filled out the report was a young man in his twenties. He inquired what we did in this office all day, other than make jokes with our tricorn hat. So we told him. He was flabbergasted.

"You write about beer? You drink beer for a living?" He took note of our little courtyard out front. "Do you drink beer out here?" His eyes were as wide as a child's in a toy store.

"Well, yes, on many Friday afternoons when the weather is good, we enjoy a beer out here, closely monitoring our BAC levels of course, so that nobody's ever approaches

0.05," I said. "And you and your friends in the force are welcome to join us any time."

~*~

After my stint in a Costa Rican jail, I've found that it always serves my interests to befriend law enforcement whenever I come across that species. He agreed to beef up cruiser patrols in the area for the next thirty days, and maybe stop by to check on us on Friday afternoons, which is a good thing because at that time a member of my staff had a rather interesting past. And by "interesting," I mean "terrifying."

Earlier that summer, I had been on the hunt for a new full-time administrative assistant for a while. If you had ever tested our live customer service around then, you knew that it often left much to be desired. My mistake was that, in an effort to conserve resources, I hired young interns who did a good job for the two months it took to train them properly, and then they left. That summer we had been particularly short-handed.

So I put out feelers. I needed somebody who was brilliant at Microsoft Windows programs, could type like a demon without making typos, could learn to work our unlearnable subscription system, never got sick, could answer the phone and help readers with their problems, could keep up with my travel and make sure I got to my destinations, and wanted to work for low pay and no benefits. Somehow we didn't have people lining up outside the door filling out applications. I blamed the local beer distributorships. They've taken all the best people who are willing to work for low wages.

Finally, I did find the perfect candidate. My friends who had offices next door own apartment complexes around town and referred her to me. She had all the qualifications — and she was a nice elderly lady with a Barcelona accent. I asked my friend why he was letting her go, and this real estate tycoon actually stammered.

"Well," he said, "uh, we ran criminal checks on all our employees and it turns out she has, er, a little bit of a past history."

What could this nice old lady have done that was so horrible, I ask? Shoplift a Rite-Aid?

Actually, no. It turns out this nice cosmopolitan lady with the Barcelona accent killed her husband with a hammer. Most people would not consider hiring her for obvious reasons, not the least of which is that, once hired, you could never fire her. It would be like having a union Jersey garbage collector in the office — lifetime employment. Quite a change from Alexandra the intern who gave us such bubbly reports of her exploits on-premise amongst co-eds.

But being a contrarian, I was tempted to give her a try. After all, she was willing to take the job, low pay and all. BeerNet has always been somewhat of an island of misfit toys. I figured we'd just have to hide the heavy tools.

"And for God's sake," I advised my subscribers, "pay your renewals on time."

~*~

The Christmas holiday wound up being fantastic after all, despite two burglaries and my questionable decision to include a convicted murderer to my staff.

Why, you may ask, do I say that my Christmas was fantastic? This brings me to the second thing that makes December the most wonderful time of the year. Two words: Pennsylvania Dutch. Given my string of bad luck, I thought it only fitting to indulge myself in that most pleasurable of holiday treats. In fact, I found that Pennsylvania Dutch was the best answer to almost every question over the holidays, to wit:

Want a drink?

ü Why yes, I'll have some Pennsylvania Dutch if you please.

Want to watch TV?
ü Yes, and be a good girl and fetch me a dram of Pennsylvania Dutch.

Want a sandwich?
ü No, I'm saving the calories for a Touch of the Dutch.

Want some breakfast?
ü Sure. Well, on second thought, pour me a tumbler of P-Dutch instead, will ya?

Do you know where my sunglasses are?
ü I thought you'd never ask, but yes I'd love a tall glass of cold Pennsylvania Dutch.

What is Pennsylvania Dutch? You grind up half an elf, capture the seed after pleasuring a reindeer, toss in a pair of Santa's drawers, put it in a blender, have it blessed by an Amish elder, and Pennsylvania Dutch is what you get on the other end.

Actually it's three-quarters bottom-shelf brandy, rum, and bourbon (that quality control at any self-respecting distillery would normally pour down the drain) mixed with one-fourth slightly curdled cream, and that's Pennsylvania Dutch. So naturally, it's absolutely delicious. It's like Zeus is peeing in your mouth. The minute Thanksgiving comes around I start buying it up by the case, because it goes fast in my town.

The only question when having a Touch o' the Dutch is: neat or on the rocks? My rule of thumb is to always drink P-Dutch neat before noon, as if it were a glass of milk or, say, a vitamin shake; and on the rocks after noon, as then it's more of a cocktail. But those are just my rules. I don't pay the mortgage at your house, so you can make your own rules. What's great about the Dutch is it's an appropriate aperitif at any time of day. Or at least it is at my house, where I'm the one paying the mortgage.

And P-Dutch is a versatile mixer too — it allows you get in touch with your creative side, if you have one. If you don't, drink sixteen ounces of the Dutch and you will. Diageo kindly sent me a bottle of Godiva chocolate-infused vodka, which is more like Aphrodite peeing in your mouth. You put a shot of that into a moderately clean glass, top it off with some P-D, and voila! You have what I call the Flying Dutchman. Two shots of vodka and it's called the Headless Dutchman. Three shots, Vomiting Dutchman. Add a banana and blend, the Kraaaazy Dutchman ("He's gone toootally bananas!!" Badda-bing). Add chocolate syrup and blend, the Tan Dutchman: An Oxymoron Drink (alternatively called "Dutch Chocolate" or "Dutch West

Indies"). Add sauerkraut and blend, the Boer (do not recommend). Add strawberries and blend, the Fairy Dutchman - It's Fabulous! Forget to put the top on the blender and it leaks all over the place, which we call The Julian Assange Wiki-Dutch (har-de-har-har). And so on.

But be warned: Too much Pennsylvania Dutch and you will soon be "going Dutch" on dates on Match.com because your spouse will have left you. There's nothing quite so pathetic as somebody who is prostrate and debauched on Dutch. But it's almost worth it.

Farewell, O. Henry's

I WAS IN AUSTIN recently for a niche publishers' conference – a seminar for niche trade publishers to better themselves. Since I could use some self-improvement, I attended. Turns out we were already doing most of the things they taught, so it was more of a lesson in validation.

I stayed at the Hilton downtown, on 4th and Neches. This hotel is new – well, let's put it this way: it wasn't there when I went to college in Austin twenty-five years ago. But from the moment I walked into the lobby, I had a weird feeling that I couldn't shake. Like I'd been there before. Something familiar about the place, but I couldn't put my finger on it.

Until I looked out the window of the second-story conference room and saw the little bungalow once owned by O. Henry, the turn-of-the-century iconic writer who briefly lived in Austin in that tiny home until he stole from the bank he worked at and was uncharitably run out of town. The sight of it literally stopped me in my tracks, because the one thing I remember about O. Henry's house is that it was directly across the street from O. Henry's Back Forty Bar, the honky-tonk I practically lived at during my later college days. We spent so much time there that the bar's owner, Louis, set up tabs for us so we could pay her once at the end of every month. We went there so much that Louis was invited to my wedding. We went there so much that Louis would often find us sitting on the front step in the afternoon, waiting for her to open it up at three. We spent so much time there that it is the only bar my wife Lulu has been kicked out of, twice. (Lulu and Louis didn't get along very well as I remember it).

It was a run-down bar in a rock house that probably should have been condemned years ago. Half the house was a barbecue restaurant and half was O. Henry's Back Forty. Sometimes, when the wind came from a certain direction, smoke from the restaurant's fire pit would fill O. Henry's and our clothes smelled of pork sausage for days (but it had the benefit of clearing the fleas out of O. Henry's carpets and drapes). I always loved how the bar stole for its name two diametrically opposite themes: a literary satirical writer and an expression from a cowboy show on TV. The irony wouldn't be lost on O. Henry himself. In fact the "O. Henry's" part of the sign fell down at some point so newbies only knew it as – simply – the Back Forty. Only veterans like myself knew that it was really called "O. Henry's Back Forty," or sometimes we called it Oh B-F. I think it was originally called O. Henry's and then Louis added "Back Forty" to give it more street cred with college kids, most of whom went to public school and so had no idea who O. Henry was.

Anyway, as soon as I saw O. Henry's house I took the elevator down and walked across the street to make sure I wasn't wrong (I wasn't). Then I looked back at the Hilton, an imposing structure, on the very spot where O. Henry's Back Forty should be. What the hell?

So I rang my old friend Jeff Smith, who also frequented Oh B-F so much that he sometimes was confused with the furniture.

Me: "Jeff, it's Harry. What the f— happened to O. Henry's?"

Jeff: "You mean the Back Forty?"

Me: (sighing impatiently)

Jeff: "Didn't you know? Louis sold the real estate to Hilton for three million dollars. She bought a Dodge sports car, which she called 'Baby Car' and then died."

Isn't that always what happens? Poor Louis wanted to be "Big Rich" (as she put it) for all her life and finally achieves that dream on the back of Conrad Hilton and then doesn't live long enough to properly enjoy "Baby Car."

Incidentally, I knew that Jeff would know the story. He always kept up with the "bar characters" we befriended while in college: the bartender/bookie/pimp Richard, No-Neck the tire guy, the drunken state senator who had to be carried home most nights, and the barmaid Bev whom we all scandalously made out with at various times (without regret, I insist). When I left Austin I left the characters behind and didn't look back. Not Jeff. Jeff is a loyal friend to the end, even to bar characters. I think he even sent Bev a TV as a congratulatory gift when her son was released from prison.

So now O. Henry's Back Forty is a fancy glass and steel convention hotel. They call that progress. I call it bullshit.

Please Come to Boston

One of the speakers at my first "Annual" Beer Industry Summit was Mark H. Rodman of Beverage Distribution Consultants. I wondered why Mark did not attend my 2006 summit, but he was undergoing a relatively minor surgery. I am sad to report that Mark's heart unexpectedly gave out during that surgery, and my good friend died on that operating table.

I returned to Boston to attend his funeral. I stayed at the Eliot Hotel, naturally, on the corner of Mass Ave and Commonwealth, in Boston's Back Bay neighborhood. The hotel is just across the street from the tiny apartment Lulu and I used to live in, with two babies and a dog, fifteen years ago while I attended classes across the river.

One night we took the babies and the dog for a walk and got locked out of our apartment. We had no money and no phone, not that we could have called anybody because we also had no friends in Boston. It was getting cold so we ducked into the lobby of the Eliot Hotel, and the nice people who worked there graciously let us stay in a room (dog and all) and called a locksmith to get us back into our apartment. I later wrote a letter to the hotel's management telling them that for the rest of my life, every time I return to Boston I will stay at the Eliot Hotel; I'm sure if they had known that, they wouldn't have been so generous. Luckily, it's a nice hotel. It would have been unfortunate if a youth hostel or drug-soused seedy motel had taken us in.

Here's the thing about Boston: Nothing ever changes. The city itself is so old that change is viewed askance by its provincial and suspicious peoples. Even that tunnel they dug under the Charles River took twenty years to complete. And not to be too unkind, but Bostonians are such an unfortunate-looking lot. It's like they keep a chain-link fence around the city to keep the ugly people in, so they don't escape and spread their bad genes across the country. It almost throws me into a depression when I'm there ... I look at national underwear catalogues on the subway just to keep from throwing myself onto the third rail. And they all wear moth-eaten wool hats and cheap nylon Red Sox jackets and they all have chronic bed head. What's up with that? A friend suggested it's because it's so cold that people don't want to shower in the morning. I told her, "You know, Chicago's cold too, but they don't all have bed head." Another theory blown out of the water by your editor's superior intellect.

Boston also has the most Dunkin' Donut stores of any place on earth. There's one on every corner; it's almost ridiculous. They love them some Dunkin' Donuts in Beantown. There may be some sort of correlation between the Dunkin' Donuts, the chronic bed head, and the general fugliness of Bostonians, but I haven't cracked the code yet. But I feel I'm close. I'll spend another two days contemplating something that is completely irrelevant.

I had a few hours to kill so I decided to follow my daily route of fifteen years ago and took the Red Line over the Charles River to Cambridge. I sat sandwiched between two ugly people with moth-eaten wool hats, cheap nylon Red Sox jackets, and bed head, as they ate their Dunkin' doughnuts.

I walked around the Harvard campus and eventually ended up at my old watering hole, the John Harvard Brewpub, where your hair must be neatly washed and combed to get service. I had a clam chowder, a Scottish ale, and worked on the next day's issue of BBD. I must admit it was very satisfying, because I had originally kind of conceived of BBD in that very pub. To sit at the bar ten years later with an actual business doing what I love is ... well, I'm very lucky.

It was a melancholy sort of day — we buried Mark — but it was an ephemeral trip back to younger and poorer days for me, sort of bittersweet. After the funeral we trekked out to Swampscott, Mark's hometown, a little fishing village on the Atlantic, and drank beer at Red Rock's Bistro, a glass-walled and light-filled restaurant on the water. It was Mark's favorite.

I spoke for a long while with Jerry Steinman, the former publisher of *Beer Marketer's Insights*. He is such a character and very vibrant for his eighty-plus years. I asked him how he was doing, and he said, "Harry,

I'm alive, I'm healthy, my family's healthy, I've got some money in the bank ... it could be worse." Amen to that. I did not tell him this, but years ago at a National Beer Wholesalers Association convention, he was such a rock star to me that I followed him up an escalator and tried to gather the nerve to introduce myself, but ultimately chickened out.

I told Mark's widow, Kathy, that I had a voice recording of an interview I did with Mark a few months ago, and if she desired I would send her a copy. Poor Kathy broke down and cried at this. I hope Lulu, or really any pretty girl, cries at my wake. Kathy thanked me for coming from so far away. I told her that Mark would have come down for mine, and besides, if you don't go to people's funerals, they won't come to yours. She nodded with a curious expression and moved on to other, more sane, people.

I Can't See

There's been a particular development in my life that has affected all other parts of my everyday existence: I can't see. I've never been able to see far — been wearing the glasses since grade school for that. But over the last year or so it has developed that I can't see up close, even, and especially with, my glasses. Phone, wristwatch, remote control … forget about it, can't see it. ATM machine screens, gas pump readers, credit card numbers, nope. Papers on my desk, car keys, stuff in my center console. Can't see it. Menus, receipts, restaurant checks, phone bills, elephants … well, you get the picture.

One surprise benefit: I've abdicated any responsibility for almost everything smaller than a couch under the auspices that I can't be held responsible for things I can't see.

~*~

All of this had caused me to review my life and start making changes – changes of the "let's make everything bigger and simpler" type. I gave the Rolex I received as a gift from my grandmother in 1995 to my oldest son, Harrison, and bought a Timex with big numbers that's backlit. I changed the font sizes on my computer and phone. I hand bar tabs to whomever I'm with, feigning complete ignorance of what to do next, in the hopes that they'll either pay or at least fill out my tip for me. I bought an iPad and have started using that instead of my phone.

I've started to extricate from my life anything that's smaller than a loaf of bread. That's my standard. If it can fit in a breadbox, it goes in the trash. Sometimes it's unavoidable. In hotel showers, instead of taking the trouble of reading the tiny print on the little bottles, I'll just play hair-wash roulette. Eeny meeny miney mo, I wonder how my hair will go. Yes, sometimes my hair smells like Listerine and sometimes it smells like lavender body lotion, but screw it. My hair's all falling out anyway so it won't matter anymore soon enough.

Ruling out the possibility that I've been bitten by a spider and will soon develop super powers, I can only assume it's going to get worse. But you know I don't complain. Okay, I complain incessantly. So everybody keeps saying to get bifocals. Seriously? I'm forty-five, not eighty. I suppose I can get reading glasses, but that's just one more thing for me to keep up with. My cycle with things I absolutely need — glasses, keys, phone, wallet—goes something like this: Have --> Lose --> $Replace$ --> Find. I don't need yet another item to get caught up in that expensive and aggravating vortex. So I will do as others have done before me, endeavor to persevere.

LEAVING LAS VEGAS

I TOOK MY TWO oldest sons, whom I call Dinkus and Bonehead, to Las Vegas over Labor Day weekend to show them the largest golden nugget in the world. Taking children to Vegas is a tricky maneuver. They can't gamble, drink, or whore. So you make do. I knew the largest golden nugget in the world, while a spectacle to behold, would not hold their young ADD minds for long, being an inanimate rock and all.

To keep them occupied with other non-rock-related activities in Sin City, I padded our agenda with shows by two talented old mensches doing their last run on the Vegas circuit before they retire or die. The first was David Copperfield, the greatest illusionist to walk the face of the earth, according to Oprah, who would know. As a boy I remember him being very serious and dramatic—and good at making sexy times with the ladies, or as good at making sexy times with a lady as a magician can reasonably be. A man's sexy-time ability is directly proportional to the thickness of his chest hair and his willingness to expose that chest hair, and Copperfield was sporting a bear rug from neck to navel. Besides, making the Statue of Liberty disappear and reappear is, after all, a serious and sexy business.

But in his later years he apparently did what all of us middle-aged men do—turn to humor. The show was goofy and funny, something I didn't expect. He did bring me and a few others on stage so he could make us disappear (sorry, he swore us to secrecy on how he does the trick). Afterwards we met him backstage. He truly is a master, but his eyes were weary from performing the same tricks on the same audience for five hundred shows a year.

The second night, we saw another open-collared, hairy-chested legend of the '70s—Neil Diamond. We (including me) were easily the youngest people there by twenty years. Next to us was an old man who was obviously deeply moved by the performance. After the third song he was in tears. By mid-show he was bawling. By the time Neil was singing some old Barbra Streisand ballad the old man had to be led out by his wife. I don't entirely blame him. It was supposedly Neil's last concert, and this guy had seen him at the "Hot August Night" concert in '72. It was a heartrending moment. By the way, you'll be glad to know that Neil still has it, even at seventy-one. The man still has more talent and testosterone in his little pinky than most men have in their entire bodies, and a full head of hair. The show was simply fantastic.

On Saturday we let one of my oldest girl friends, whom I call Fancy, take us to fancy lunch at the Bellagio and then let us go on the private balcony of her fancy employer to watch the fancy fountains. Very fancy. Fancy is so fancy that I dare not mention her real name or her employer, as she would surely be fired for even being acquainted with somebody so un-fancy as I.

But as fancy as Fancy is, I coerced her into taking us downtown so that I could show my sons the infamous golden nugget. Leaving the fanciness of the strip to go downtown, where the stairs in the parking garages double as urinals, was a tough sell to

Fancy, but I eventually prevailed, and even got her to take a picture in front of a poster of a busty nurse holding a twenty-four ounce PBR and declaring proudly, "I like it in the can." You can take Fancy out of Beaumont, but Beaumont, I find, sticks to you like tar, and it's a tough thing to shake.

But the best part of the trip was to be found on the plane ride home. The outbound flights from Vegas are always great for spotting train wrecks that make you feel better about yourself. There was a pretty girl across the aisle who looked like holy hell, a real hot mess. Thick brown hair with cheap chunky highlights piled up carelessly in a chip clip, sunglasses on, skinned knees, mysterious brown stains on her shirt, slugging her third Bloody Mary — last night's makeup a fading smudge betraying a helluva good time — a younger, hung-over Sarah Palin if you will. She catches me watching her, and I expect her expression to say, "I don't give a fuck what you think of me," but what it actually says is, "Damn I could really use a cigarette." I consider offering her one of my Nicorette lozenges, but then think the better of it; she's the type of girl who thinks nicotine tablets are for pussies and she's right. She pulls out a tattered copy of … is it *Fifty Shades of Gray*?

No, not for our party girl. *The Rum Diaries* by Hunter Thompson. I am a little bit in love with her. I imagine she's a ball of fun when she wants to be, and a real bitch all other times. In other words, the type of girl I'm as likely as not to fall in love with.

She seems to want to talk to the middle-aged man next to her, but the dude is unresponsive. It's infuriating. I don't know what's being pumped through this goofball's Bose headphones, but I guarantee it's not as interesting as learning our girl's story. If I were her seatmate, I would be peppering her with probing questions and indulging myself in her sordid life (all the while congratulating myself on my relative respectability, naturally). I'd learn about her wild bachelorette weekend in Vegas, how she got her bra caught in the pool drain at the Luxor, how the bride's fiancé is a cheating asshole, about her ex-boyfriend's addiction to *Call of Duty*, about her dead-end job as a hostess at Macaroni Grill, about how she's three credits short of graduating from Addison Community College, and her lifelong dream to someday be a pediatric nurse. About her father's early death from an ironworking accident, and how she's currently not on speaking terms with her mother because she let her cat Mysty out and it got run over. I would invite her to come to the ranch for Thanksgiving, and my wife and sisters would disapprove after she gets into the wine and swims topless in the pond at midnight with our dog Biscuit. I would learn about all these things and more, and we would become good friends, calling each other late at night to hash out her problems. I would advise her to forgive her mother — Mysty would have wanted it that way — and I would lend her the money to fly to Reno for their tearful reunion. Her mother would come to the ranch the next Thanksgiving, and it would emerge that she is a licensed massage therapist specializing in gout, and she works her magic and cures my sore ankles ... and so on.

These are the fantasies I spin to pass the time on planes when you can't turn on your iPad because you have yet to reach ten thousand feet at the time (which is a stupid rule, by the way, and I'm glad the idiots at the FAA finally saw the light). For all I know she is getting her PhD in solid rocket fuel and was in Vegas to give a speech to NASA. But I prefer my party girl version, in need of an older savior, a respectable businessman who can guide her to her dream of being an RN.

I follow her off the plane at DFW, and she walks flat-footed, toes out like a duck in her flip-flops with sparkly sequins. My heart swells; it's an endearing effect. I'll never see her again of course, and she will be forever unaware of her wannabe guardian angel.

--

DRAGONS LIVE FOREVER, BUT NOT SO LITTLE BOYS

I HAVE THREE SONS, twenty-one, nineteen, and fourteen. It seems like just yesterday that the oldest was in Kindergarten. My wife Lulu cried on his first day. And I laughed it off because, after all, he'd be in Kindergarten for a full year. Today I look at him and he's a senior in college, and my middle boy is also in college, and my baby is starting to drive. Now I'm the one crying.

I still have one little bear. My little one and I are very close. The reason is because I started my business twenty years ago, and when you're self-employed you can take random days off on a whim. I took several afternoons off to take Wywy to a movie or to the ranch. He's a snuggler, so on many nights I would crash in his bed and we would talk about the day, or sharks, or the different types of zombies, or battleships. Those days are drawing nigh as he gets older and realizes that snuggling with your daddy isn't cool anymore, if it ever was.

It brings to mind the song, "Puff the Magic Dragon":

A Dragon lives forever, but not so little boys.
Painted wings and giant's rings make way for other toys.
One gray night it happened, Jackie Paper came no more.
And Puff that mighty dragon, he ceased his fearless roar.
His head now bent in sorrow, green scales fell like rain.
Puff no longer went to play, along that cheery lane.
Without his life-long friend, Puff could not be brave,
So Puff that mighty dragon sadly slipped into his cave.

It's true. The little boys we knew suddenly, quite miraculously and with no notice, grow up. We wake up one day to find our little boys all big and using deodorant and calling girls and going out. This has proved too much for me to handle. The last time I bawled this much was the 2002 Budweiser ad commemorating 9/11.

The commentator Rich Galen wrote a great post on this a few years ago, pointing out that with regard to children growing up, there are two types of people in this world: those who get it and those who don't. I get it. My baby bear is soon to be no more, and it just breaks my heart. He's about to be gone forever, only to be retrieved in the recesses of my besotted memory and the few pics and videos that survive the never-ending iPhone syncs.

In fact, I'm so proud of the young men my boys have become, but I still dearly miss the little boys — the ones who marveled at trains, airplanes, and helicopters; the ones who called hamburgers hangubers; the ones who will race into your arms for a hug after school — those little boys are no more. I can't go on, my keyboard is wet.

ABOUT THE AUTHOR

Harry Schuhmacher is the founder, editor and publisher of *Beer Business Daily*, *Wine and Spirits Daily*, and *Craft Business Daily*.
He lives in San Antonio.

Made in the USA
San Bernardino, CA
02 April 2016